Percy FitzPatrick

Jock of the Bushveld

Illustrated by E. Caldwell

Edited by Linda Rosenberg

AD. DONKER/PUBLISHER

AD DONKER (PTY) LTD
A DIVISION OF JONATHAN BALL PUBLISHERS (PTY) LTD
P O Box 33977
Jeppestown
2043

First published in this edition 1989
Reprinted 1990, 1993, 1997, 1999

ISBN 0 86852 176 0 (Hardback)
ISBN 0 86852 177 9 (Paperback)

Cover design by Michael Barnett
Typeset by M.M. Fourie, Johannesburg
Printed and bound byNational Book Printers, Drukkery Street,
Goodwood, Western Cape

Contents

Editor's Note

This South African classic among animal stories is published here in a shortened version in which the language has been modernised for better readability. While the prejudicial racial references have been eliminated, the esoteric charm and innocent philosophical tone have been left scrupulously intact.

Dedication

It was the youngest of the High Authorities
who gravely informed the Inquiring
Stranger that
'Jock Belongs to the Likkle People!'
That being so, it is clearly the duty, no
less than the privilege, of the
Mere Narrator to
Dedicate
The Story of Jock
to
Those Keenest and Kindest of Critics, Best
of Friends, and Most Delightful
of Comrades
The Likkle People

Preface

To an audience of little people a story may be told a hundred times, but it must be told, as Kipling says, 'Just so!' that is, in the same way, because, even a romance must be true to itself.

Once Jock had taken the field it was not long before the narrator found himself helped or driven over the pauses by quick suggestions from the gallery. But there were days of fag and worry when thoughts lagged or strayed, and when slips were made, and then a vigilant and pitiless memory swooped like the striking falcon on its prey.

There came a night when the story was of the old crocodile, and one in the gallery — one of more exuberant fancy — seeing the gate open ran into the flower-strewn field of romance and by suggestive questions and eager promptings helped to gather a little posy: 'And he hung on and fought him, didn't he?' 'And the old crocodile flung him high into the air? High!' and, turning to the two juniors, added 'quite as high as the house!' And the narrator — accessory by reason of a mechanical nod and an absent-minded yes — passed on, thinking it could all be put right next time. But there is no escape when the little people sit in judgement. It was months later when retribution came. The critical point of the story was safely passed when in solemn protest a hand was laid on the narrator's shoulder and a reproachful voice said 'Dad! You have left out the best part of all. Don't you remember how . . .'

From the date of that lesson it was apparent that reputations would suffer if the story of Jock were not speedily embodied in some durable and authoritative form.

The story belongs to the little people, and their requirements were defined — 'It must be *all true*! Don't leave out *anything*!' It has been necessary to leave out a great deal, but the other condition has been fully and fairly complied with. It is a true story from beginning to end. It is not a diary. Incidents have been grouped and moved to get over the difficulty of blank days and bad spells, but there is no incident of importance or of credit to Jock which is not absolutely true. The severest trial in this connection was in the last chapter, which is bound to recall perhaps the most famous and most cherished of all dog stories. Much, indeed, would have been sacrificed to avoid that; but it was unthinkable that, for any reason, one should in the last words shatter the spell that holds Jock dear to those for whom his life is chronicled — the spell that lies in 'a true story'.

The Background

Of the people who live lonely lives, on the veld or elsewhere, few do so of their own free choice. Some are shut off from their kind — souls sheathed in some invisible film through which no thrill of sympathy may pass Some, barred by their self-consciousness, never learned in childhood to make friends. Some have a secret or a grief, thoughts too big or bad for comradeship.

Go out among them. Who can know what they think, or dream, or hope, or suffer?

Yet something you may guess, since with the man there often goes — his dog; his silent tribute to The Book. Oh, it's little they know of life who cannot guess the secret springs of loneliness and love that prompt the keeping of a trifling pet so that in the trackless miles of wilderness a man feels he has a friend. Something to hold on to, something to protect.

There was a boy who went to seek his fortune. Call him a boy or man, the years proved nothing either way. Some will be boyish always; others were never young: a few — most richly endowed few — are man and boy together. He went to seek his fortune, as boys will and should. For life was easy there, and all was pleasant, as it may be in a cage. Today is sure and happy and there is no tomorrow in a cage.

11

There were friends enough — all kind and true — and in their wisdom they said, 'Here it is safe, yonder all is chance, where many indeed are called, but few are chosen. Many have gone forth and only few are free and well. But the few are those who count, and lead, and those who follow do not think, 'How few', but 'How strong! How free!''

There was something that strove within him; that grew and grew, and beat and fought for freedom; that bade him go and walk alone and tell his secret on the mountain slopes to one who would not laugh — a little red retriever that made him climb and feel his strength, and find an outlet for what drove within.

So the boy set out to seek his fortune, and did not find it; for there was none in the place where he sought. Time and place and things had failed him but the effort was right. And, when that was clear beyond all question, it was instinct and not knowledge bade him still go on, saying, 'Not back to the cage. Anything but that!'

Rough and straight-spoken, but kindly men and true, were those he came among. What they could they did: what they had they gave. They made him free of board and bed; and, kinder still, now and then made work for him to do, knowing his spirit was as theirs and that his heart cried out, 'Not charity, but work. Give me work.' But that they could not do, for there was no work they could not do themselves. They did not even ask his name; it made no difference.

Thus the days and weeks went by, until the day when the little child that lies hidden in us all reached out — as in the dark — for a hand to hold; and there was none. His arms went up to hide the mocking glory of the day, and face buried in the grass, he sobbed, 'Not worth my food!'

Science tells that Nature will recoup herself by ways as well defined as those that rule mechanics. Whatever

impulse sways the guiding hand, we know that often when we need it most there comes relief; gently, unbidden, unobserved.

A wisp of drifting cloud came by, a breath of cooler air, and the fickle spirit of the mountain changed the day as with a wand. The boy woke up shivering, dazed, bewildered. The cold driving mist had blotted out the world. Stronger and stronger grew the wind, driving the damp cold through and through, for on the bleak plateau of the mountain nothing broke its force.

Pale and shaken, and a little stiff, he looked about, then slowly faced the storm. It had not struck him to turn back.

The gusts blew stronger, and through the mist came rain, in single stinging drops. Slowly, as he bent to breast it, the chilled blood warmed, and when the first thunderclap split overhead, and lost itself in endless roars and rumblings in the kloofs and hills around, there came a warmth about his heart and a light into his eye — mute thanksgiving that here was something he could battle with and be a man again.

The boy pressed on — the little path a racing stream to guide him. In a group of ghostly, mist-blurred rocks he stopped to drink, and, as he bent — for all the blackness of the storm — his face leaped out at him reflected for one instant in the shallow pool. The blue-white flame of lightning, blinding his aching eyes, hissed down. The sickening smell of brimstone spread about, and crashing thunder close above his head left him dazed and breathless.

Heedless of the rain, blinking the blackness from his eyes, he sat still waiting for his head to clear, and for his limbs to feel their life again. And, as he waited, slowly there came upon a colder stiller air that other roar, so weird and terrifying — the voice of the coming hail.

Huddled beneath the shelving rock he watched the storm sweep by with an awful battering din that swamped and silenced every other sound.

The dense packed column of hail swept along, ruthless, raging, and unheeding, overwhelming all until there was a sudden failing of its strength, a little straggling tail, and then — the silence.

13

The sun came out, the wind died down. Light veils of mist came slowly by and melted in the clear, pure air.

The boy stepped out once more. Miles away the black column of the falling hail sped its appointed course. Under his feet, where all had been so green and beautiful, was battered turf, for the time transformed into a mass of dazzling brilliants.

On the glittering surface many things stood out.

In the narrow pathway near the spring, a snake lay on its back, crushed and broken. Beyond it was a tortoise, not yet dead, but bruised and battered. Further afield lay something reddish-brown — a buck — the large eyes glazed, an ooze of blood upon its lips and nose. He stooped to touch it, but drew back: the dainty little thing was pulp.

All striving for the sheltering rocks. All caught and stricken by the ruthless storm. And he, going on to face it, while others fled before — he, blindly fighting on — was spared. Was it luck? Or was there something subtle, more? He held to this, that more than chance had swayed the guiding hand of fate — that fortune holds some gifts in store for those who try. 'It is good to be alive! But . . . better *so* than in the cage.'

Once more, a little of the fortune that he had come to seek.

At sunset, passing down the long rough gorge, he came upon a transport-rider battling with the flood. The mad bewildered oxen were yielding to the stream and heading, with the wagons, downwards towards the falls. In their utmost need the boy swam in and helped. And there, at last, the boy was worth his food.

14

Into the Bushveld

'Distant hills are always green', and the best gold further on. That is a law of nature — human nature — which is quite superior to facts; and thus the world moves on.

So from the Lydenburg gold-fields prospectors 'humping their swags' or driving their small pack-donkeys spread afield, and transport-riders with their long spans and rumbling wagons followed, cutting a wider track where traders with winding strings of carriers had already ventured on. But the hunters had gone first. There were great hunters whose names are known. Others as great who missed the accident of fame, and after them hunters who traded, and traders who hunted. And so too with prospectors, diggers, transport-riders and all.

Between the gold-fields and the nearest port lay the bushveld, and game enough for all to live on. Thus, all were hunters of a sort, but the great hunters — the hunters of big game — were apart; we were the smaller fry, there to admire and to imitate.

Perched on the edge of the Drakensberg, we overlooked the wonder-world of the bushveld, where the big game roamed in thousands. Living on the fringe of a hunter's paradise, most of us were drawn into it from time to time, for shorter or longer spells, as opportunity and our circumstances allowed. Little by little one got to know the names, appearances, and habits of the many kinds of game. In the quiet nights there were long talks under the wagons, in the grass shelters in the woods, or in the wattle-and-daub shanties of the diggers. Here I learned to understand something of the man we knew simply as Rocky, and here I first heard of Jim Makokel'.

Jim was a Zulu wagon-driver who had worked for one of our party — Bob Saunderson. 'We came right on to a lioness waiting for us, and I got her', said Bob one night when it was his turn to provide our 'nights' entertainment, 'and then there were shouts, and I saw a couple of cubs, pretty well grown, making off in the grass. This driver, Jim, legged it after one of them, a cub about as big as a Newfoundland dog. I followed as fast as I could, but he was a big Zulu and went like a buck, yelling like mad all the time. We were in the bend of one of the long pools down near the Komati, and when I got through the reeds

the cub was at the water's edge facing Jim, and Jim was dancing around heading it off with only one light stick. As soon as it saw us coming on, the cub took to the water, and Jim after it. It was as good as a play. Jim swam up behind, and putting his hand on its head ducked it right under. The cub turned as it came up and struck out at him viciously, but he was back out of reach. When it turned again to go Jim ducked it again, and it went on like that six or eight times, till the thing was half drowned and had no more fight in it. Then Jim got hold of it by the tail and swam back to us, still shouting and quite mad with excitement.

'Of course, you can say it was only a cub; but it takes a

good man to go up naked and tackle a thing with teeth and claws that can cut you into ribbons.'

'Was Jim here today?' I asked, as soon as there was an opening. Bob shook his head with a kindly regretful smile. 'No, sonny, not here; you'd have heard him. Jim's gone. I had to sack him. A real fine worker, but a terror to drink, and always in trouble. He wore me out.'

We were generally a party of half a dozen — the owners of the four wagons, a couple of friends trading with Delagoa Bay, a man from Swaziland, and Rocky, an old Yankee hunter-prospector. It was our holiday time, before the hard work with loads would commence, and we dawdled along feeding up the cattle and taking it easy ourselves.

It was too early for loads in Delagoa Bay so we moved slowly and hunted on the way, sometimes camping for several days in places where the grass and water were good.

Game there was in plenty, but it did not come my way. Days went by with, once or twice, the sight of some small buck just as it disappeared, and many times the noise of something in the bush or the sound of galloping feet. Others brought their contributions to the pot daily, and there seemed to be no reason in the world why I alone should fail — no reason except sheer bad luck! It is difficult to believe you have made mistakes when you do not know enough to recognise them, and have no idea of the extent of your own ignorance; and then bad luck is such an easy and such a flattering explanation.

If I did not go so far on the easy road of excuse-making as to put all the failures down to bad luck, perhaps Rocky deserves the credit.

One evening as we were lounging round the camp fire, Robbie, failing to find a soft spot for his head on a thorn log, got up reluctantly to fetch his blankets, exclaiming with a mock tragic air:

> The time is out of joint; O cursed spite,
> That ever I was born to set it right.

We knew Robbie's way. There were times when he would

17

spout heroics suggested by some passing trifle, his own face a marvel of solemnity the whole time, and only the amused expression in his spectacled grey eyes to show he was poking fun at himself. An indulgent smile, a chuckle, and the genial comment 'Silly ass!' came from different quarters, for Robbie was a favourite. Only Old Rocky maintained his usual gravity.

As Robbie settled down again in comfort, the old man remarked in level thoughtful tones, 'I reckon the feller who said that was a waster, he chucked it!' There was a short pause in which I, in my ignorance, began to wonder if it was possible that Rocky did not know the source; or did he take the quotation seriously? Then Robbie answered in mild protest, 'It was a gentleman of the name of Hamlet who said it.'

'Well, you can bet he was no good, anyhow', Rocky drawled out.

'A man who blames his luck is no good.'

'You don't believe in luck at all, Rocky?' I ventured to put in.

'I don't say there's no such thing as luck — good and bad. But it isn't the explanation of success and failure — not by a long way. When another man pulls off what you don't, the first thing you've got to believe is it's your own fault, and the last, it's his luck. And you've just got to wade in and find out where you went wrong, and put it right, without any excuses and explanations.'

'But, Rocky, explanations aren't always excuses, and sometimes you really have to give them.'

'Sonny, you can be dead sure there's something wrong about a thing that doesn't explain itself. One explanation's as bad as two mistakes — it doesn't fool anybody except yourself.'

I was beaten. It was no use going on, for I knew he was right. I suppose the other fellows also knew whom he was getting at, but they said nothing, and the subject seemed to have dropped, when Rocky, harking back to Robbie's quotation, said, with a ghost of a smile, 'I reckon if Hamlet had to keep the camp in meat we'd go hungry.'

Rocky had no fancy notions. He hunted for meat and got it as soon as possible. He was seldom out long, and rarely indeed came back empty-handed. I had already learnt not to be too ready with questions. It was better, so Rocky put it, 'to keep your eyes open and your mouth shut'. But the results at first hardly seemed to justify the process. At the end of a week of failures and disappointments all I knew was that I knew nothing — a very notable advance it is true, but one quite difficult to appreciate.

The only dog with us was licking a cut on her shoulder — the result of an unauthorised rush at a wounded buck — and after an examination of her wound we had wandered over the account of how she had got it, and so on to discussing the dog herself. Rocky was in silence, smoking and looking into the fire, and the little discussion was closed by someone saying, 'She's no good for a hunting dog — too plucky!' It was then I saw Rocky's eyes turned slowly on the last speaker. He looked at him thoughtfully for a good minute, and then remarked quietly, 'There is no such thing as too plucky'. And with that he stopped, almost as if inviting contradiction. Whether he wanted a reply or not one cannot say; anyway, he got none. No one took Rocky on unnecessarily, and at his leisure he resumed: 'She's no fool, but she hasn't been taught. Men have got to learn, dogs too. Boys are like pups — you've got to help them but not too much, and not too soon. They've got to learn themselves. I reckon if a man's never made a mistake he's never had a good lesson.'

My eyes were all for Rocky, but he was not looking my

way, and when the next remark came, and my heart jumped and my hands and feet moved of their own accord, his face was turned quite away from me towards the man on his left.

'It's just the same with hunting. It looks so easy a boy reckons it doesn't need any teaching. Well, let him try. Mostly you've got to make a fool of yourself once or twice to know what it feels like and how to avoid it. Best to do it young — it teaches a boy; but it kind of breaks a man up.'

The old man paused, then naturally and easily picked up his original point, and turning another look on Jess, said, 'You got to begin on the pup. It isn't her fault; it's yours. She's full of the right stuff, but she's got to learn. Dogs are all different, good and bad — just like men: some learn quick; some'll never learn. But there aren't any too plucky!'

He tossed a chip of green wood into the heart of the fire and watched it spurtle and smoke, and after quite a long pause, added, 'There's times when a dog's got to see it through and be killed. It's his duty — same as a man's. I've seen it done!'

The last words were added with a narrowing of his eyes and a curious softening of voice — as of personal affection or regret. Others noticed it too; and in reply to a question as to how it had happened Rocky explained in a few words that a wounded buffalo had waylaid and tossed the man over its back, and as it turned again to gore him the dog rushed in between, fighting it off for a time and eventually fastening on to the nose when the buffalo still pushed on. The check enabled the man to reach his gun and shoot the buffalo; but the dog was trampled to death.

'Were you . .?' someone began — and then at the look in Rocky's face, hesitated. Rocky, staring into the fire, answered, 'It was my dog.'

Long after the other men were asleep I lay in my blankets watching the tricks of light and shadow played by the fire, as fitfully it flamed or died away. I could not sleep, but Rocky was sleeping like a babe. He, gaunt and spare — 1,8 metres he must have stood — weather-beaten and old,

with a long solitary trip before him and sixty-odd years of
life behind, he slept when he laid his head down, and was
wide awake and rested when he raised it. He, who had been
through it all, slept. But I, who had only listened, was haunted,
bewitched, possessed by racing thoughts, and all on account
of four words, and the way he said them: 'It was my dog'.

It was still dark, with a faint promise of saffron in the
east, when I felt a hand on my shoulder and heard Rocky's
voice saying, 'Comin' along, sonny?'

One of the drivers raised his head to look at us as we
passed. He called to his voorloper to turn the cattle loose to
graze, and dropped back to sleep.

What is there to tell of that day? Why, nothing, really
nothing, except that it was a happy day — a day of little
things that all went well, and so it came to look like the
birthday of the hunting. It was all too beautiful for words
as it should be in the springtime of youth.

Rocky was different that day. He pointed out the spoors
going to and from the drinking-place, and named the various
animals. He showed me one spoor more deeply indented than
the rest and, murmuring 'Scared I guess', pointed to where it
had dashed off out of the regular track. He stopped quietly in
his stride to point where a hare was sitting up cleaning itself,
not 9 metres off. Stopped again at the sound of a clear,
almost metallic 'clink' and pointed to a little sandy gully
in front of us down which presently came thirty or forty
guinea-fowl in single file moving swiftly, in absolute silence
except for that one 'clink'. How did he know they were
there, and which way they would go, and know it all so
promptly, were questions I asked myself.

We came to a patch of old long grass and I got out in
time to see a rietbuck ram cantering away. Rocky gave a
shrill whistle, the buck stopped, side on, looked back at
us, and Rocky dropped it where it stood. Instantly following the shot there was another rush on our left, and
before the second rietbuck had gone 27 metres Rocky
toppled it over in its tracks. From the whistle to the second
shot it was all done in about ten seconds. To me it looked
like magic. I could only gasp.

We cleaned the bucks, and hid them in a bush. There

21

was meat enough for the camp then, and I thought we would return at once, but Rocky, after a moment's glance round, shouldered his rifle and moved on again. I followed, asking no questions.

A quarter of an hour later Rocky stopped, subsided to a sitting position, beckoned to me, and pointed with his levelled rifle. It was a couple of minutes before he could get me to see the stembuck standing in the shade of a thorn tree. I would never have seen it but for his whisper to look for something moving.

Rocky laid his hand on my shoulder: 'Take your time, sonny', he said, 'aim low; and *don't pull! Squeeze!*' And at last I got it.

We had our breakfast there — the liver roasted on the coals, a couple of 'doughboys', and the unexpected addition of a bottle of cold tea, weak and unsweetened, produced from Rocky's knapsack. I realised that of his deliberate kindliness Rocky had come out that morning meaning to make a happy day of it for a youngster, and he did it.

We stayed there a couple of hours and he really opened out. He had the knack of getting to the heart of things, and putting it all in the fewest words. He spoke in the same slow grave way, with habitual economy of breath and words, and yet the pictures were living and real, and each incident complete. I seemed to get from him that morning all there was to know of the hunting in two great continents.

That was a happy day.

When I woke up next morning Rocky was fitting the packs on his donkeys. I was a little puzzled, wondering at first if he was testing the saddles, for he had said nothing about moving on. But when he joined us at breakfast the donkeys stood packed ready to start. Robbie asked, 'Going to make a move, Rocky?'

'Yes.' He answered quietly.

I ate in silence, thinking of what he was to face. Many hundreds of kilometres — perhaps a thousand or two; many, many months — maybe a year or two; wild country, wild tribes, and wild beasts; floods and fever; accident, hunger, and disease; and alone.

When we had finished breakfast he rinsed out his beaker and hung it on one of the packs, slung his rifle over his shoulder, and picking up his long walking-stick tapped the donkeys lightly to turn them into the footpath that led away north.

Rocky paused a second before following, turned one brief grave glance on us, and said: 'Well. So long.' He never came back.

Jess

Good dogs were not easy to get, I had tried hard enough for one before starting, but without success.

Good hunting dogs were rare; as rare as good men, good horses, and good front oxen. A lot of qualities are needed in the make-up of a good hunting dog: size, strength, quickness, scent, sense and speed — and plenty of courage.

There was only the one dog in our camp, and she was not an attractive one. She was a bull-terrier with a dull brindled coat — black and grey in shadowy stripes. She had small cross-looking eyes and uncertain always-moving ears. She was bad-tempered and most unsociable, but she was as faithful and as brave a dog as ever lived. She never barked, never howled when beaten for biting strangers, and she was silent, savage and very quick. She belonged to my friend Ted, and never left his side day or night. Her name was Jess.

Jess was not a favourite, but everybody respected her. She was not a hunting dog, but on several occasions she had helped to pull down wounded game. She had no knowledge or skill, and was only fierce and brave, so there was always the risk that she would be killed. She would listen to Ted, but to no one else. One of us might have shouted his lungs out, but it would not have stopped her from giving chase the moment she saw anything and keeping on till she was too dead beat to move any further.

The first time I saw Jess we were having dinner, and I gave her a bone — putting it down close to her and saying, 'Here! Good dog.' As she did not even look at it, I moved it right under her nose. She gave a low growl, and her little eyes turned on me for just one look as she got up and walked away.

There was a snigger of laughter from some of the others, but nobody said anything, and it seemed wiser to ask no questions just then. Afterwards, when we were alone, one of them told me Ted had trained her not to feed from any one else, adding, 'You must not feed another man's dog; a dog has only one master.'

We respected Jess greatly, but no one knew quite how much we respected her until the memorable day near Ship Mountain.

We had rested through the heat of the day under a big tree on the bank of a little stream. About sundown, just before we were ready to start, some other wagons passed, and Ted, knowing the owner, went on with him, intending to rejoin us at the next outspan. As he jumped on to the passing wagon he called to Jess. She answered his call instantly, but when she saw him moving off on the other wagon she sat down in the road and for some seconds watched him anxiously. She ran on a few steps in her curious quick silent way and again stopped, giving swift glances alternately towards Ted and towards us. Ted remarked laughingly that she evidently thought he had made a mistake by getting on to the wrong wagon, and that she would follow presently.

After he had disappeared she ran back to her patch of grass and lay down, but in a few minutes she was back again squatting in the road looking with that same anxious worried expression after her master. Thus she went to and fro for the quarter of an hour it took us to inspan, and each time she passed we could hear a faint anxious little whine.

The oxen were inspanned and the last odd things were

25

being put up when one of the wagon drivers came to say that he could not get the guns and water-barrel because Jess would not let him near them. There was something the matter with the dog, he said; he thought she was mad.

We laughed at the notion, and went for the things ourselves. As we came within five yards of the tree where we had left the guns there was a rustle in the grass, and Jess came out with her swift silent run, appearing as unexpectedly as a snake does. Her head, body and tail were in a dead line, and she was crouching slightly as for a spring. Her ears were laid flat back, her lips twitching constantly, showing the strong white teeth, and her cross wicked eyes had such a look of remorseless cruelty in them that we stopped as if we had been turned to stone. She never moved a muscle or made a sound, but kept those eyes steadily fixed on us.

We moved back a pace or two and began to coax and wheedle her, but it was no good. For a minute we stood our ground, and then the hair on her back and shoulders began very slowly to stand up. That was enough: we cleared off.

Another tried his hand; but it was just the same. No one could do anything with her; no one could get near the guns or the water-barrel. As soon as we returned for a fresh attempt she reappeared in the same place and in the same way.

We turned to watch her as she ran back for the last time, and as she disappeared in the grass we heard distinctly the cry of a very young puppy. The secret of Jess's madness was out.

We had to send for Ted, and when he returned a couple of hours later Jess met him out on the road. She jumped up at his chest giving a long tremulous whimper of wel-

come, and then ran ahead straight to the nest in the grass.

He took a lantern and we followed, but not too close. When he knelt down to look at the puppies she stood over them and pushed herself in between him and them. When he put out a hand to touch them she pushed it away with her nose, whining softly in protest and trembling with excitement — you could see she would not bite, but she hated him to touch her puppies. Finally, when he picked one up she gave a low cry and caught his wrist gently, but held it.

That was Jess, the mother of Jock.

The Pick of the Puppies

There were six puppies, and as the wagons were empty we fixed up a roomy nest in one of them for Jess and her family. There was no trouble with Jess; nobody interfered with her, and she interfered with nobody. We used to look at her and the puppies as we alked along with the wagons, so by degrees she got to know that we would not harm them, and she no longer wanted to eat us alive if we went near and talked to her.

Five of the puppies were fat strong yellow little chaps with dark muzzles — just like their father. Their father was an imported dog, and was always spoken of as the best dog of the breed. I never saw him, so I do not really know what he was like — perhaps he was not a yellow dog at all, but, whatever he was, he had at that time a great reputation because he was 'imported', and there were not half a dozen imported dogs in the whole of the Transvaal.

It seemed rough on her that every one was glad there was only one puppy like the mother — the sixth one, a poor miserable little rat of a thing about half the size of the others. He was not yellow like them, nor dark brindled like Jess, but a sort of dirty pale half-and-half colour with some dark faint wavy lines all over him, as if he had tried to be brindled and failed; and he had a dark sharp wizened little muzzle that looked shrivelled up with age.

Most of the fellows said it would be a good thing to drown the odd one because he spoilt the litter and made them look as though they were not really thoroughbred, and because he was such a miserable little rat that he was not worth saving anyhow. But in the end he was allowed to live. I believe no one fancied the job of taking one of Jess's puppies away from her. Moreover, as any dog was better than none, I had offered to take him rather than let him be drowned. Ted had old friends to whom he had already promised the pick of the puppies, so when I came along all he could promise me was that if there should be one over I might have it.

As they grew older and were able to crawl about they were taken off the wagons when we outspanned and put on the ground. Jess got to understand this at once, and she used to watch us quite quietly as we took them in our hands to put them down or lift them back again. When they were two or three weeks old a man came to the wagons who talked a great deal about dogs, and appeared to know what had to be done. He said that the puppies' tails ought to be docked, and that a bull-terrier would be no class at all with a long tail, but that you should on no account clip his ears. We found out afterwards that he had made a mistake, but it was too late then, and Jess's puppies started life as bull-terriers with long ears and short tails.

I felt sure from the beginning that all the yellow puppies would be claimed and that I should have to take the odd one, or none at all, so I began to look after him. I felt sorry for him, too, because he was small and weak, and the other five big puppies used to push him away from his food and trample on him. When they were old enough to play they used to pull him about by his ears and pack on to him — three or four to one — and bully him horribly. Many a time I rescued him, and many a time gave him a little preserved milk and water with bread soaked in it when the others had shouldered him out and eaten everything.

After a while I began to notice little things about him that no one else noticed, and got to be quite fond of the little beggar. Perhaps I grew fond of him simply because he was lonely and had no one else to depend on. Perhaps it was because he was always cheerful and plucky and it seemed as if there might be some good stuff in him after all. The other puppies would tumble him over and take his food. They would bump into him when he was stoop-

29

ing over the dish of milk and porridge, and his head was
so big and his legs so weak that he would tip up and go
heels over head into the dish. We were always picking him
out of the food and scraping it off him.

One day just after the wagons had started, I took a
final look round the outspan place to see if anything had
been forgotten and I found the little chap — who was only
about 10 centimetres high — struggling to walk through the
long grass. He was not big enough or strong enough to push
his way — even the stems of the downtrodden grass tripped
him. He stumbled and floundered at every step, but he got up
again each time with his little tail standing straight up, his
head erect, and his ears cocked.

What he thought he was doing, goodness only knows.
He looked as proud and important as if he owned the whole
world and knew that every one in it was watching him. The
poor little chap could not see a metre in that grass, and in
any case he was not old enough to see or understand much,
but he was marching along as full of confidence as a general
at the head of his army.

How he fell out of the wagon no one knew, but the
others were a bit more softened towards the odd puppy
when I caught up to the wagons and told them of his
valiant struggle to follow, and the man who had docked
the puppies' tails allowed, 'I believe the rat's got pluck,
whatever else is the matter with him, for he was the only
one that didn't howl when I snipped them.' But no one
else said a good word for him: he was really beneath notice,
and if they ever had to speak about him they called him 'the
Rat'.

There is no doubt about it he was extremely ugly, and

instead of improving as he grew older, he became worse; yet I could not help liking him and looking after him. Sometimes I felt sorry for him, sometimes I was tremendously amused, and sometimes — wonderful to relate — I really admired him. He was extraordinarily silent. While the others barked at nothing, howled when lonely, and yelled when frightened or hurt, the odd puppy did none of these things. In fact, he began to show many of Jess's peculiarities. He hardly ever barked, and when he did it was not a wild excited string of barks but little suppressed muffled noises, half bark and half growl, and just one or two at a time. He did not appear to be afraid of anything, so one could not tell what he would do if he was.

One day we had an amusing instance of his nerve. One of the oxen, sniffing about the outspan, caught sight of him all alone, and filled with curiosity came up to examine him. It moved towards him slowly and heavily with its ears spread wide and its head down, giving great big sniffs at this new object, trying to make out what it was. The Rat stood quite still with his stumpy tail cocked up and his head a little on one side. When the huge ox's nose was about 30 cm from him he gave one of those funny abrupt little barks. It was as if the object had suddenly 'gone off' like a cracker, and the ox nearly tumbled over with fright. Even when the great mountain of a thing gave a clumsy plunge round and trotted off, the Rat was not the least frightened. He was startled, and his tail and ears flickered for a second, but they stiffened up again instantly, and with another of those little barks he took a couple of steps forward and cocked his head on the other side. That was his way.

He was not a bit like the other puppies. If any one fired off a gun or cracked one of the big whips the five of them would yell at the top of their voices, and start running as fast as they could towards the wagon without once looking back to see what they were running from. The odd puppy would drop his bone with a start or would jump round. His ears and tail would flicker up and down for a second. Then he would slowly bristle up all over, and with his head cocked stare hard with his half-blind bluish puppy eyes in the direction of the noise, but he never ran away.

31

And so, little by little, I got to like him in spite of his awful ugliness. And it really was awful. The other puppies grew big all over, but the odd one at that time seemed to grow only in one part — his tummy. The poor little chap was born small and weak. He had always been bullied and crowded out by the others, and the truth is he was half-starved. The natural consequence of this was that as soon as he could walk about and pick up things for himself he made up for lost time, and filled up his middle piece to an alarming size before the other parts of his body had time to grow. At that time he looked more like a big tock-tockie beetle than a dog.

Besides the balloon-like tummy he had stick-out bandy legs, and a neck so thin that it made the head look enormous. But what made him so supremely ridiculous was that he evidently did not know he was ugly. He walked about as if he was always thinking of his dignity, and he had that puffed-out and stuck-up air of importance that you only see in small people and bantam cocks who are always trying to appear 2 cm taller than they really are.

When the puppies were about a month old they could feed on porridge or bread soaked in soup or gravy. Jess used to leave them for hours at a time and hide in the grass so as to have a little peace and sleep. Puppies are always hungry, so they soon began to hunt about for themselves. They would find scraps of meat and porridge or old bones, and if they could not get anything else, would try to eat the rawhide nekstrops and reims. That's when the fights began. As soon as one puppy saw another busy on anything, he would walk over towards him and, if strong enough, fight him for it. All day long it was nothing but wrangle, snarl, bark and yelp. Sometimes four or five would be at it in one scrum, because as soon as one heard a row going on he would trot up hoping to steal the bone while the others were busy fighting.

It was then that I noticed other things about the odd puppy. No matter how many packed on to him, or how they bit or pulled him, he never once let out a yelp. With four or five on top of him you would see him on his back, snapping right and left with bare white teeth, gripping and worrying them when he got a good hold of anything, and all the time growling and snarling with a fierceness that was really comical.

Before many days passed, it was clear that some of the other puppies were inclined to leave the Rat alone, and that only two of them — the two biggest — seemed anxious to fight him and could take his bones away. The reason soon became apparent. Instead of wasting his breath in making a noise, or wasting strength in trying to tumble the others over, the Rat simply bit hard and hung on. Noses, ears, lips, cheeks, feet and even tails — all came handy to him. Anything he could get hold of and hang on to was good enough, and the result generally was that in about half a minute the other puppy would leave everything and clear off.

When either of the big puppies tackled the little fellow the fight lasted much longer. Even if he were tumbled over at once — as generally happened — and the other one stood over him barking and growling, that did not end the fight. As soon

as the other chap got off him he would struggle up and begin again. He would not give in. The other puppies seemed to think there was some sort of rule like the 'count out' in boxing, or that once you were tumbled over you ought to give up the bone, but the odd puppy apparently did not care about rules. As far as I could see, he had just one rule: 'Stick to it'; so it was not very long before even the two big fellows gave up interfering with him. The bites from his little white teeth which punctured noses and feet and tore ears, were most unpleasant. But apart from that, they found there was nothing to be gained by fighting him. They might roll him over time after time, but he came back again and worried them so persistently that it was quite impossible to enjoy the bone — they had to keep on fighting for it.

At first I drew attention to these things, but there was no encouragement from the others; they merely laughed at the attempt to make the best of a bad job. Once, when I had described how well he had stood up to Billy's pup, Robbie caught up the Rat and, placing him on the table, said, 'Hats off to the Duke of Wellington on the field of Waterloo.' That seemed to me the poorest sort of joke to send five grown men into fits of laughter. He stood there on the table with his head on one side, one ear standing up, and his stumpy tail twiggling — an absurd picture of friendliness, pride and confidence; yet he was so ugly and ridiculous that my heart sank, and I whisked him away. After that I stopped talking about him.

Then there came a day when something happened which might easily have turned out very differently, and there would have been no stories and no Jock to tell about; and the best dog in the world would never have been my friend and companion. The puppies had been behaving very badly, and had stolen several nekstrops and chewed up parts of one or two big whips. The drivers were grumbling about all the damage done and the extra work it gave them, and Ted, exasperated by the worry of it all, announced that the puppies were quite old enough to be taken away, and that those who had picked puppies must take them at once and look after them, or let someone else have them.

When I heard him say that my heart gave a little thump from excitement, for I knew the day had come when the great question would be settled once and for all. Here was a glorious and unexpected chance; perhaps one of the others would not or could not take his, and I might get one of the good ones.

In the afternoon Ted came up to where we were all lying in the shade, and startled us with the momentous announcement:

'Billy Griffiths can't take his pup.'

Every man of us sat up. Billy's pup was the first pick, the champion of the litter, the biggest and strongest of the lot. Several of the others said at once that they would exchange theirs for this one, but Ted smiled and shook his head.

'No', he said, 'you had a good pick in the beginning.' He turned to me, 'You've only had leavings. You can have Billy's pup.'

It seemed too good to be true. Not even in my wildest imaginings had I fancied myself getting the pick of the lot. I hardly waited to thank Ted before going off to look at my champion. I had seen and admired him times out of number, but it seemed as if he must look different now that he belonged to me. He was a fine big fellow. Well built and strong, he looked as if he could beat all the rest put together. His legs were straight; his neck sturdy; his muzzle dark and shapely; his ears equal and well carried; and in the sunlight his yellow coat looked bright, with occasional glints of gold in it. He was indeed a handsome fellow.

As I put him back again with the others the odd puppy, who had stood up and sniffed at me when I came, licked my hand and twiddled his tail with the friendliest and most independent air, as if he knew me quite well and was glad to see me. I patted the poor little chap as he waddled up. I had forgotten him in the excitement of getting Billy's pup, but the sight of him made me think of his funny ways, his pluck and independence, and of how he had not a friend in the world except Jess and me. I picked him up and talked to him, and when his wizened little face was close to mine he opened his mouth as if laughing, and shooting out his red tongue dabbed me right on the tip of my nose in pure friendliness.

I put him back with the other puppies and returned to the tree where Ted and the rest were sitting. As I came up there was a shout of laughter, and — turning round to see what had provoked it — I found the Rat at my heels. He had followed me and was trotting and stumbling along, tripping every metre or so, but getting up again with head erect, ears cocked and his stumpy tail twiddling away.

All the old chaff and jokes were fired off at me again,

and I had no peace for quite a time. They all had something to say: 'He won't swap you off'; 'He is going to take care of you'; 'He is afraid you'll get lost'; and so on.

Billy's failure to take his puppy was so entirely unexpected and so important that the subject kept cropping up all the evening. It was very amusing then to see how each of those who had wanted to get him succeeded in finding good reasons for thinking that his own puppy was really better than Billy's. However they differed in their estimates of each other's dogs, they all agreed that the best judge in the world could not be certain of picking out the best dog in a good litter until the puppies were several months old. They all gave instances in which the best-looking puppy had turned out the worst dog, and others in which the one that no one would look at had grown up to be the champion.

I fell asleep that night thinking of the two puppies — the best and the worst in the litter. No sooner had I gone over all the splendid points in Billy's pup and made up my mind that he was certainly the finest I had ever seen, than the friendly wizened little face, the cocky little stump of a tail, and the comical dignified plucky look of the odd puppy would all come back to me. The thought of how he had licked my hand and twiddled his tail at me, how he had dabbed me on the nose, and the manful way in which he had struggled after me through the grass, all made my heart go soft towards him, and I fell asleep not knowing what to do.

When I woke up in the morning, my first thought was of the odd puppy — how he looked to me as his only friend, and what he would feel like if he knew he was to be left behind or given away to any one who would take him. From the way he had followed me the night before it was clear he was looking after me. His whole manner had plainly said, 'Never mind old man! Don't you worry, I am here.'

We used to make our first trek at about three o'clock in the morning, so as to be outspanned by sunrise, and walking along during that morning trek I recalled all the stories that the others had told of miserable puppies having grown into wonderful dogs, and of great men who had been

very ordinary children, and at breakfast I took the plunge.

'Ted', I said, bracing myself for the laughter, 'if you don't mind, I'll stick to the Rat.'

If I had fired off a gun under their noses they would have been much less startled. Robbie made a grab for his plate as it slipped from his knees.

'*Don't* do that sort of thing!' he protested indignantly. 'My nerves won't stand it!'

The others stopped eating and drinking, held their beakers of steaming coffee well out of the way to get a better look at me, and when they saw it was seriously meant there was a chorus of:

'Well, I'm hanged.'

I took him in hand at once — for now he was really mine — and brought him over to where we sat at breakfast. Beside me there was a rough camp table — a luxury sometimes indulged in while camping or trekking with empty wagons. I put the puppy and his saucer of soaked bread and milk in a safe place under the table and sank the saucer into the sand so that when he trod in it he would not spill the food, for puppies are quite as stupid as they are greedy, and seem to think that they can eat faster by getting further into the dish. He finished it all and looked round briskly at me, licking his lips and twiddling his stumpy tail.

Well, I meant to make a dog of him, so I gave him another lot. He thought he was still very hungry and could eat any amount more; but it was not possible. The lapping became slower and more laboured, with pauses every now and then to get breath or lick his lips and look about him, until at last he was fairly beaten. He could only look at it, blink and lick his chops. He was too full to move. He stood where he was, with his legs well spread and his little body blown out like a balloon, and finished licking the drops and crumbs off his face without moving 30 centimetres.

There was something so extraordinarily funny in the appearance and attitude of the puppy that we watched to see what he would do next. He had been standing very close to the leg of the table, but not quite touching it. When he finished feeding and after he had done washing his face and cleaning up generally, he stood stock still for several minutes, as though it was altogether too much trouble to move. One little bandy hind leg stuck out behind the table-leg, and the bulge of his little tummy stuck out in front of it; so that when at last he decided to make a move the very first little lurch brought his hip up against the table-leg. In an instant the puppy's appearance changed completely. The hair on his back and shoulders bristled; his head went up erect; one ear stood up straight and the other at half cock; and his stumpy tail quivered with rage. He evidently thought that one of the other puppies had come up behind to interfere with him. He was too proud to turn round and appear to be nervous. With his head erect he glared hard straight in front of him, and, with all the little breath that he had left after his big feed, he growled ferociously in comical little gasps.

After a minute's pause he calmed down and very slowly

39

and carefully began to step forward. Of course exactly the same thing happened, except that this time he shook all over with rage, and the growling was fiercer and more choky. One could not imagine anything so small being in so great a rage. He took longer to cool down, too, and much longer before he made the third attempt to start. But the third time it was all over in a second. He seemed to think that this was more than any dog could stand, and that he must put a stop to it. The instant his hip touched the leg, he whipped round with a ferocious snarl — his little white teeth bared and gleaming — and bumped his nose against the table-leg.

I cannot say whether it was because of the shout of laughter from us, or because he really understood what had happened, that he looked so foolish, but he gave one crestfallen look at me and with a feeble wag of his tail waddled off as fast as he could.

Then Ted nodded over at me, and said, 'I believe you have got the champion after all!'

And I was too proud to speak.

Jock's School-days

After that day no one spoke of the Rat or the odd puppy, or used any of the numberless nicknames that they had given him. They still laughed at his ridiculous dignity and they loved to tease him to see him stiffen with rage and hear his choky little growls, but they liked his independence and admired his tremendous pluck. So they respected his name when he got one.

And his name was Jock.

Jock got such a good advertisement by his fight with the table-leg that every one took notice of him now and remarked about what he did, and as he was only a very young puppy, they teased him, fed him, petted him, and did their best to spoil him. He was so young that it did not seem to matter, but I think if he had not been a really good dog at heart he would have been quite spoilt.

He soon began to grow and fill out, and it was then that he taught the other puppies to leave him alone. If they had not interfered with him he might perhaps have left them alone, as it was not his nature to interfere with others. But the trouble was they had bullied him so much while he was weak and helpless that he got used to the idea of fighting for everything.

It is probably the best thing that could have happened

41

to Jock that as a puppy he was small and weak, but full of pluck. It compelled him to learn how to fight; it made him clever, cool, and careful, for he could not afford to make mistakes. When he fought he meant business. He went for a good spot, bit hard, and hung on for all he was worth. As the enemy began to slacken, he would start vigorously worrying and shaking. I often saw him shake himself off his feet because the thing he was fighting was too heavy for him.

The day Jock fought the two big puppies — one after the other — for his bone, and beat them off, was the day of his independence. We all saw the tussle, and cheered the little chap. For one whole day he had peace. But it was like the pause at low water before the tide begins to flow the other way. He was so used to being interfered with that I suppose he did not immediately understand they would never tackle him again.

It took a whole day for him to realise this, but as soon as he did understand it he seemed to make up his mind that now his turn had come, and he went for the first puppy he saw with a bone. He walked up slowly and carefully, and began to make a circle round him. When he got about half-way round the puppy took up the bone and trotted off. But Jock headed him off at once, and again began to walk towards him very slowly and stiffly. The other puppy stood quite still for a moment, and then Jock's fierce determined look was too much for him. He dropped the bone and bolted.

There was mighty little but smell on those bones, for we gave the puppies very little meat, so when Jock had taken what he could off this one, he started on another hunt. A few metres away Billy's pup was having a glorious time, struggling with a big bone and growling all the while as if he wanted to let the world know that it was as much as any one's life was worth to come near him. None of us thought Jock would tackle him, as Billy's pup was still a long way the biggest and strongest of the puppies, and always ready to bully the others.

Jock was about three or four metres away when he caught sight of Billy's pup, and for about a minute he stood still and quietly watched. At first he seemed surprised, and then interested, and then gradually he stiffened up all over in that funny way of his. When the hair on his shoulders was all on end and his ears and tail were properly up, he moved forward very deliberately. In this fashion he made a circle round Billy's pup, keeping about 60 cm away from him, walking infinitely slowly and glaring steadily at the enemy out of the corners of his eyes. While he was doing this, the other fellow was tearing away at his bone, growling furiously and glaring sideways at Jock. When the circle was finished they stood once more face to face. After a short pause Jock began to move in closer, but more slowly than before.

Billy's pup did not like this. It was beginning to look serious. He could not keep on eating and at the same time watch Jock. Moreover, there was such a very unpleasant wicked look about Jock, and he moved so steadily and silently forward, that any one would feel a bit creepy and nervous. So, he put his paw on the bone and let out a string of snarly barks, with his ears flat on his neck and his tail rather low down. But Jock still came on — a little more carefully and slowly perhaps, but just as steadily as ever. When about 30 cm off the enemy's nose he changed his direction slightly, as if to walk past, and Billy's pup turned his head to watch him, keeping his nose pointed towards

Jock's, but when they got side by side he again looked straight in front of him.

Perhaps he did this to make sure the bone was still there, or perhaps to show his contempt when he thought Jock was going off. Whatever the reason was, it was a mistake, for, as he turned his head away, Jock flew at him, got a good mouthful of ear, and in no time they were rolling and struggling in the dust. Jock's little grunts were barely audible in the noise made by the other one. Billy's pup was big and strong, and he was not a coward, but Jock was worrying his ear vigorously, and he could not find anything to bite in return. In less than a minute he began to howl, and was making frantic efforts to get away. Then Jock let go the ear and tackled the bone.

After that he had no more puppy fights. As soon as any one of the others saw Jock begin to walk slowly and carefully towards him he seemed to suddenly get tired of his bone, and moved off.

One by one the other puppies were taken away by their new masters, and before Jock was three months old he and Jess were the only dogs with the wagons. Then he went to school, and like all schoolboys learnt some things very quickly — the things that he liked; and some things he learnt very slowly, and hated them. When I poked about with a stick in the banks of dongas to turn out mice and field-rats for him, or when I hid a partridge or a hare and made him find it, he was as happy as could be. But when I made him lie down and watch my gun or coat while I pretended to go off and leave him, he did not like it, and as for his lessons in manners, well, he simply hated them.

There are some things which a dog in that sort of life simply must learn or you cannot keep him. The first of these is, not to steal. Every puppy will help himself until

44

he is taught not to. Your dog lives with you and can get at everything. At the outspan the grub-box is put on the ground, open for each man to help himself. If you make a stew, or roast the leg of a buck, the big three-legged pot is put down handy and left there. If you are lucky enough to have some tinned butter or condensed milk, the tins are opened and stood on the ground; and if you have a dog thief in the camp, nothing is safe.

There was a dog with us once — a year or two later — who was the worst thief I ever knew. He was a one-eyed pointer with feet like a duck's, and his name was Snarleyow. The first bad experience I had of Snarley was on one of the little hunting trips which we sometimes made in those days, away from the wagons. We travelled light on those occasions, and, except for some tea and a very little flour and salt, took no food. We lived on what we shot and of course kept 'hunter's pot'.

Hunter's pot is a perpetual stew; you make one stew, and keep it going as long as necessary, maintaining a full pot by adding to it as fast as you take any out. Scraps of everything go in; any kind of meat — buck, bird, pig, hare — and if you have such luxuries as onions or potatoes, so much the better. To make the soup strong, the big bones are added — the old ones being fished out every day and replaced by a fresh lot. When allowed to cool it sets like brawn, and a hungry hunter wants nothing better.

We had had a good feed the first night of this trip and had then filled the pot up, leaving it to simmer as long as the fire lasted, expecting to have cold pie set in jelly — but without the piecrust — for early breakfast next morning.

To our amazement, in the morning the pot was empty.

That night we made the fire close to our sleeping-place, but next morning the pot was again empty — cleaned and polished as if it had been washed out. While we, speechless with astonishment and anger, were wondering who the thief was and what we should do with him, one of the hunters came up and pointed to the prints of a dog's feet in the soft white ashes of the dead fire. Snarleyow. The thief was lying fast asleep comfortably curled up on his master's clothes. There could be no mistake about those big splayed footprints, and in about two minutes Snarleyow was getting a first-class hammering, with his head tied inside the three-legged pot for a lesson.

After that he was kept tied up at night, but Snarleyow was past curing. We had practically nothing to eat but what we shot, and nothing to drink but bush tea — that is, tea made from a certain wild shrub with a very strong scent. It is not nice, but you drink it when you cannot get anything else. We could not afford luxuries. But two days before Ted's birthday we sent a runner off to Komati Drift and bought a small tin of ground coffee and a tin of condensed milk for his birthday treat. Because it was to be a real feast that day, he cut the top off the tin instead of punching two holes and blowing the milk out, as we usually did. What we could not use in the coffee that day we were going to spread on our doughboys instead of butter and jam. It was to be a real feast.

The five of us sat down in a circle and began on our hunter's pot, saving the good things for the last. While we were still busy on the stew, there came a pathetic heart-breaking yowl from Snarleyow, and we looked round just in time to see him, his tail tucked between his legs and his head

46

high in the air, bolting off into the bush as hard as he could lay legs to the ground, with the milk tin stuck firmly on to his nose. The greedy thief, in trying to get the last scrap out had dug his nose and top jaw too far in, and the jagged edges of the tin had gripped him. The last we saw of our birthday treat was the tin flashing in the sunlight on Snarley's nose as he tore away into the bush.

Snarleyow came to a bad end. His master shot him as he was running off with a ham. He was a full-grown dog when he came to our camp, and too old to learn principles and good manners.

I taught Jock not to touch food in camp until he was told to 'take it'. The lesson began when he got his saucer of porridge in the morning. He must have thought it cruel to have that put in front of him, and then to be held back or tapped with a finger on the nose each time he tried to dive into it. At first he struggled and fought to get at it, then he tried to back away and dodge round the other side. He became dazed, and, thinking it was not for him at all, wanted to walk off and have nothing more to do with it. In a few days, however, I got him to lie still and take it only when I patted him and pushed him towards it, and in a very little time he got on so well that I could put his food down without saying anything and let him wait for permission. He would lie down with his head on his paws and his nose right up against the saucer, so as to lose no time when the order came; but he would not touch it until he heard 'Take it'. He never moved his head, but his little browny dark eyes, full of childlike eagerness, used to be turned up sideways and fixed on mine. I believe he watched my lips; he was so quick to obey the order when it came.

When he grew up and had learned his lessons there was no need for these exercises. He got to understand me so well that if I nodded or moved my hand in a way that meant 'all right', he would go ahead. By that time he was also dignified and patient. It was only in his puppyhood that he used to crouch up close to his food and tremble with impatience and excitement.

There was one lesson that he hated most of all. I used to

47

balance a piece of meat on his nose and make him keep it there until the word to take it came. Time after time he would close his eyes as if the sight of the meat was more than he could bear, and his mouth would water so from the savoury smell that long streels of dribble would hang down on either side.

It seems unnecessary and even cruel to tantalise a dog in that way, but it was not, it was education, and true kindness. It taught him to understand his master, and to be obedient, patient, and observant. It taught him not to steal. It saved him from much sickness, and perhaps death, by teaching him not to feed on anything he could find. It taught him manners and made it possible for him to live with his master and be treated like a friend.

Good feeding, good care, and plenty of exercise soon began to make a great change in Jock. He ceased to look like a beetle and grew bigger everywhere. His neck grew thick and strong, his legs straightened up and he filled out with muscle.

There was one other change which came more slowly and seemed to me much more wonderful. After his morning feed, if there was nothing to do, he used to go to sleep in some shady place. I remember well one day watching him as he lay. His bit of shade had moved away and left him in the bright sunshine. As he breathed his ribs rose and fell and the tips of the hairs on his side and back caught the sunlight and shone like polished gold. The wavy dark lines seemed more distinct and darker, but still very soft. In fact, I was astonished to see that in a certain light Jock looked quite handsome.

Jock had many things to learn besides the lessons he got from me — the lessons of experience which nobody could teach him. When he was six months old — just old enough, if he had lived in a town, to chase a cat and make a noise — he knew many things that respectable puppies twice his age who stay at home never get a chance of learning.

On trek there were always new places to see, new roads to travel, and new things to examine, tackle or avoid. He learnt something fresh almost every day. He learnt, for instance, that, although it was shady and cool under the wagon, it was not good enough to lie in the wheel track, not even for the pleasure of feeling the cool iron tyre against your back or head as you slept; and he knew that, because one day he had done it, and the wheel had gone over his foot. Fortunately the sand was soft and his foot was not crushed, but he was very lame for some days, and had to travel on the wagon.

He learnt a good deal from Jess: among other things, that it was not necessary to poke his nose up against a snake in order to find out what it was. He knew that Jess would fight anything, and when one day he saw her back hair go up and watched her sheer off the footpath wide into the grass, he did the same. When we had shot the snake, both he and Jess came up very very cautiously and sniffed at it, with every hair on their bodies standing up.

He found out for himself that it was not a good idea to turn a scorpion over with his paw. He tried it once and was a very sick dog for some days, but after that whenever he saw a thing that he did not understand, he would watch it very carefully from a little way off and notice what it did and what it looked like, before trying experiments.

So little by little, Jock got to understand plenty of things that no town dog would ever know, and he got to know by instinct whether a thing was dangerous or safe, even though he had never seen anything like it before. That is how he knew when wolves or lions were about — and that they were dangerous. You may well wonder how he could tell whether a scent or a cry belonged to a wolf which he must avoid, or to a buck which he might hunt, when he had never seen either a wolf or a buck at the time. But he did know. He also

49

knew that no dog could safely go outside the ring of the camp fires when wolf or lion was about. I have known many town dogs that could scent them just as well as Jess or Jock could, but having no instinct of danger they went out to see what it was, and of course they never came back.

I used to take Jock with me everywhere so that he could learn everything that a hunting dog ought to know, and above all things to learn that he was my dog, and to understand all that I wanted to tell him. So while he was still a puppy, whenever he stopped to sniff at something new or to look at something strange, I would show him what it was. But if he stayed behind to explore while I moved on, or if he fell asleep and did not hear me get up from where I had sat down to rest, or went off the track on his own account, I used to hide away from him on top of a rock or up a tree and let him hunt about until he found me.

At first he used to be quite excited when he missed me, but after a little time he got to know what to do and would sniff along the ground and canter away after me — always finding me quite easily. Even if I climbed a tree to hide from him he would follow my track to the foot of the tree, sniff up the trunk as far as he could reach standing up against it, and then peer up into the branches. If he could not see me from one place, he would try another — always with his head tilted a bit on one side. He never barked at these times, but as soon as he saw me, his ears would drop, his mouth open wide with the red tongue lolling out, and the stump of a tail would twiggle away to show how pleased he was. Sometimes he would give a few little whimpery grunts; he hardly ever barked, so when he did I knew there was something worth looking at.

Jock was not a quarrelsome dog, and he was quick to learn and very obedient, but in one connection I had great difficulty with him for quite a time. He had a sort of private war with the fowls, and it was due to the same cause as his war with the other puppies. They interfered with him. Now, every one knows what a fowl is like. It is impudent, inquisitive, selfish, always looking for something to eat, and has no principles. The fowls tried to steal Jock's food, and he would not stand it. His way of dealing with them was not good for their health. Before I could teach him not to kill, and before the fowls would learn not to steal, he had finished half a dozen of them one after another with just one bite and a shake.

In the end he learnt to tumble them over and scare their wits out without hurting them, and they learned to give him a very wide berth.

I used always to keep some fowls with the wagons, partly to have fresh meat if we ran out of game, but mainly to have fresh eggs, which were a very great treat. As a rule it was only when a hen turned obstinate and would not lay that we ate her. I used to have one old rooster, whose name was Pezulu, and six or eight hens. The hens changed from time to time — as we ate them — but Pezulu remained.

Pezulu got his name by accident — in fact, by a misunderstanding. It is a Zulu word meaning 'up' or 'on top', and when the fowls first joined the wagons and were allowed to wander about at the outspan places, the drivers would drive them up when it was time to trek again by cracking their big whips and shouting 'Pezulu'. In a few days no driving or whip-cracking was necessary. One of the drivers would shout 'Pezulu' three or four times, and they would all come in and one by one fly and scramble up to the coop. One day, after we had got a new lot of hens, a stranger happened to witness the performance. The stranger, hearing the boys call 'Pezulu' and seeing him hurry up so promptly, remarked, 'How well he knows his name.' So we called him Pezulu after that.

Jock was beginning to fancy that he knew a good deal, and like most young dogs was very inquisitive and wanted to know everything and at once. He was still much inclined to poke his nose in or rush on to things instead of sniffing round about first.

However, he learnt to be careful, and an old hen helped to teach him. The hens usually laid their eggs in the coop because it was their home. But sometimes they would make nests in the bush at the outspan places. One of the hens had done this, and the bush she had chosen was very low and dense. No one saw the hen make the nest and no one saw her sitting on it, for the sunshine was so bright everywhere else, and the shade of the bush so dark that it was impossible to see anything there. But while we were at breakfast, Jock, who was bustling about everywhere, must have scented the hen or have seen this brown thing in the dark shady hole.

The hen was sitting with her head sunk right down into her

chest, so that he could not see any head, eyes or beak — just a sort of brown lump. Suddenly we saw Jock stand stock-still, cock up one ear, put his head down and his nose out, hump up his shoulders a bit and begin to walk very slowly forward in a crouching attitude. He lifted his feet so slowly and so softly that you could count five between each step. We were all greatly amused and thought he was pointing a mouse or a locust, and we watched him.

He crept up until he was only 15 cm from the object, giving occasional cautious glances back at us to attract attention. Just as he got to the hole the hen let out a vicious peck on the top of his nose and at the same time flapped over his head, screaming and cackling for dear life. It was all so sudden and so surprising that she was gone before he could think of making a grab at her, and when he heard our shouts of laughter he looked as foolish as if he understood all about it.

The First Hunt

Jock's first experience in hunting was on the Crocodile River. In the summer when the heavy rains flood the country the river runs 'bank high', hiding everything — reeds, rocks, islands and stunted trees. In some places it is silent and oily like a huge gorged snake, in others foaming and turbulent as an angry monster.

In the rainless winter when the water is low and clear the scene is not so grand, but is quiet, peaceful, and much more beautiful. There is an infinite variety in it then — the river sometimes winding along in one deep channel, but more often forking out into two or three streams in the broad bed.

There is always good shooting along the rivers in a country where water is scarce. Partridges, bush-pheasants and stembuck were plentiful along the banks and among the thorns, but the reeds themselves were the home of thousands of guinea-fowl, and you could also count on duiker and rietbuck as almost a certainty there. If this were all, it would be like shooting in a well-stocked cover, but it is not only man that is on the watch for game at the drinking places. The beasts of prey — lions, leopards, hyenas, wild dogs and jackals, and lastly pythons and croco-diles — know that the game must come to water. They lie in wait near the tracks or the drinking places. That is what makes the mystery and charm of the reeds; you never know what you will put up. The lions and leopards had deserted the country near the main drifts and followed the big game into more peaceful parts, but the reeds were still the favourite shelter and resting-place of the crocodiles and there were any number of them left.

There is nothing that one comes across in hunting more horrible and loathsome than the crocodile; nothing that rouses the feeling of horror and hatred as it does. Nothing that so surely and quickly gives the sensation of 'creeps in the back' as the noiseless apparition of one in the water just where you least expected anything, or the discovery of one silently and intently watching you with its head resting flat on a sand-spit — the thing you had seen half a dozen times before and mistaken for a small rock. Many things are hunted in the bushveld, but only the crocodile is hated. There is always the feeling that this hideous, cowardly cruel thing will

mercilessly drag you down — down — down to the bottom of some deep still pool, and hold you there till you drown. Utterly helpless yourself to escape or fight, you cannot even call, and if you could, no one could help you there. It is all done in silence. A few bubbles come up where a man went down and that is the end of it.

We were spending a couple of days on the river bank to make the most of the good water and grazing. All through the day someone or other would be out pottering about among the reeds, gun in hand, to keep the pot full and have some fun, and although we laughed and chaffed I fancy we were all very much on the look-out for rocks that looked like crocs and crocs that looked like rocks.

One of the most difficult lessons that a beginner has to learn is to keep cool. The keener you are the more likely you are to get excited and the more bitterly you feel the disappointments. Once you lose your head, there is no

55

mistake too stupid for you to make, and the result is another good chance spoilt. The great silent bush is so lonely; the strain of being on the look-out all the time is so great; the uncertainty as to what may start up — anything from a partridge to a lion — is so trying that the beginner is wound up like an alarm clock and goes off at the first touch.

On a later trip we had with us a man who was out for the first time, and when we came upon a troop of kudu he started yelling, war-whooping and swearing at them, chasing them on foot and waving his rifle over his head. When we asked him why he, who was nearest to them, had not fired a shot, all he could say was that he never remembered his rifle or anything else until they were gone.

These experiences had been mine, some of them many times, in spite of Rocky's example and advice, and they were always followed by a fresh stock of good resolutions.

I had started out this day with the same old determination to keep cool. Jock was with me, as usual. I always took him out even then — not for hunting, because he was too young, but in order to train him. He was quite obedient and kept his place behind me, and, although he trembled with excitement when he saw or heard anything, he never rushed in or moved ahead of me without permission. The guinea-fowl tormented him that day. He could scent and hear them, and was constantly making little runs forward, half-crouching and with his nose back and tail dead level and his one ear full-cocked and the other half-up.

For about half an hour we went on in this way. There was plenty of fresh duiker spoor to show us that we were in a likely place, one spoor in particular being so fresh in the mud that it seemed only a few minutes old. We were following this one very eagerly but very cautiously. It was evident that Jock agreed with me that the duiker must be near, for he took no more notice of the guinea-fowl, and I for my part forgot all about crocodiles and suspicious-looking rocks. There was at that moment only one thing in the world for me, and that was the duiker.

We crept along noiselessly in and out of the reeds, round rocks and mud holes, across small stretches of firm mud or soft sand, so silently that nothing could have heard us,

and finally we came to a very big rock, with the duiker spoor fresher than ever going close round it downstream. The rock was a long sloping one, polished smooth by the floods and very slippery to walk on. I climbed it in dead silence, peering down into the reeds and expecting every moment to see the duiker.

The slope up which we crept was long and easy, but that on the downstream side was much steeper. I crawled up to the top on hands and knees, and raising myself slowly, looked carefully about, but no duiker could be seen. Jock was sniffing and trembling more than ever, and it was quite clear that he thought we were very close up. Seeing nothing in front or on either side, I stood right up and turned to look back the way we had come and examine the reeds on that side. In doing so a few grains of grit crunched under my foot, and instantly there was a rush in the reeds behind me. I jumped round to face it, believing that a crocodile was grabbing at me from behind, and on the polished surface of the rock my feet slipped and shot from under me, both bare elbows bumped hard on the rock, jerking the rifle out of my hands; and I was launched like a torpedo right into the mass of swaying reeds.

When you think you are tumbling on to a crocodile there is only one thing you want to do — get out as soon as possible. How long it took to reach the top of the rock again, goodness only knows! It seemed like a lifetime, but the fact is I was out of those reeds and up that rock in time to see the duiker as it broke out of the reeds, raced up the bank, and disappeared into the bush with Jock tearing after it as hard as ever he could go.

One call stopped him, and he came back to me looking very crestfallen and guilty, no doubt thinking that he had behaved badly and disgraced himself. But he was not to blame at all. He had known all along that the duiker was

there — having had no distracting fancies about crocodiles
— and when he saw it dash off and his master instantly
jump in after it, he must have thought that the hunt had
at last begun and that he was expected to help.

After all that row and excitement there was not much
use in trying for anything more in the reeds — and indeed
I had had quite enough of them for one afternoon. So, we
wandered along the upper banks and it was not long before
we were interested in something else and able to forget
all about the duiker.

Before we had been walking many minutes, Jock raised
his head and ears and then lowered himself into a half-
crouching attitude and made a little run forward. I looked
promptly in the direction he was pointing and about two
hundred metres away saw a stembuck standing in the shade
of a mimosa bush. It was so small and in such bad light that
the shot was too difficult for me at that distance, and I
crawled along behind bushes, antheaps and trees until we
were close enough.

The ground was soft and sandy, and we could get along
easily enough without making any noise, but all the time,
whilst I was thinking how lucky it was to be on ground so
soft for the hands and knees, and so easy to move on without
being heard, something else was happening. With my eyes
fixed on the buck I did not notice that the muzzle of the rifle
dipped regularly into the sand, picking up a little in the barrel
each time. There was not enough to burst the rifle, but the
effect was surprising. Following on a painfully careful aim,
there was a deafening report that made my head reel and
buzz. The kick of the rifle on the shoulder and cheek left me
blue for days, and when my eyes were clear enough to see
anything the stembuck had disappeared.

I was too disgusted to move, and sat in the sand rubbing
my shoulder and thanking my stars that the rifle had not
burst. There was plenty to think about, to be sure, and no
hurry to do anything else, for the noise of the shot must
have startled every living thing for a kilometre round.

It is not always easy to tell the direction from which
a report comes when you are near a river or in broken country
or patchy bush, and it is not an uncommon thing to find that

a shot which has frightened one animal away from you has startled another and driven it towards you. That is what happened in this case.

As I sat in the shade of the thorns with the loaded rifle across my knees there was the faint sound of a buck cantering along in the sand. I looked up, and only about twenty metres from me a duiker came to a stop, half-fronting me. There it stood looking back over its shoulder, and listening intently, evidently thinking that the danger lay behind it. It was hardly possible to miss that; and as the duiker rolled over, I dropped my rifle and ran to make sure of it.

Of course, it was against the rules to leave the rifle behind, but it was simply a case of excitement again. When the buck rolled over everything else was forgotten. I knew the rule perfectly well — reload at once and never part with your gun.

Unfortunately I did not remember it when it would have been useful. As I ran forward the duiker stumbled, struggled and rolled over and over, then got up and made a dash, only to dive head foremost into the sand and somersault over. The bullet had struck it in the shoulder, and the broken leg was tripping it and bringing it down. But, in far less time than it takes to tell it, the little fellow found out what was wrong, and was off on three legs at a pace that left me far behind. Jock, remembering the mistake in the reeds, kept his place behind me, and I in the excitement of the moment neither saw nor thought of him until the duiker, gaining at every jump, looked like vanishing for ever. Then I

remembered and, with a frantic wave of my hand, shouted, 'After him, Jock.'

He was gone before my hand was down, and faster than I had ever seen him move, leaving me ploughing through the heavy sand far behind. Past the big bush I saw them gain, and there the duiker did as wounded game so often do: taking advantage of cover it changed direction and turned away for some dense thorns. But that suited Jock exactly. He took the short cut across to head it off and was close up in a few more strides. He caught up to it, raced up beside it, and made a jump at its throat. The duiker, however, darted away in a fresh direction, leaving him metres behind. Again he was after it and tried the other side; but the buck was too quick, and again he missed and overshot the mark in his jump. He was in such deadly earnest he seemed to turn in the air to get back again and once more was close up — so close that the flying heels of the buck seemed to pass each side of his ears. He made his spring from behind, catching the duiker high up on one hind leg, and the two rolled over together, kicking and struggling in a cloud of dust. Time after time the duiker got on its feet, trying to get at him with its horns or to break away again. But Jock, although swung off his feet and rolled on, did not let go his grip.

What with the hot sun, the heavy sand, and the pace at which we had gone, I was so pumped that I finished the last hundred metres at a walk, and had plenty of time to see what was going on. But even when I got up to them the struggle was so fierce and the movements so quick that for some time it was not possible to get hold of the duiker to finish it off.

At last came one particularly bad fall, when the buck rolled over on its back. Jock let go his grip and made a dash for its throat. Again the duiker was too quick for him. With one twist it was up and round facing him on its one knee, and dug, thrust and swept with its black spiky horns so vigorously that it was impossible to get at its neck. As Jock rushed in the head ducked and the horns flashed round so swiftly that it seemed as if nothing could save him from being stabbed through and through. But his quickness and cleverness were a revelation to me. If he could not catch the

60

duiker, it could not catch him. They were in a way too quick for each other, and they were a long way too quick for me.

Time after time I tried to get in close enough to grab one of the buck's hind legs, but it was not to be caught. While Jock was at it fast and furious in front, I tried to creep up quietly behind — but it was no use. The duiker kept facing Jock with horns down, and whenever I moved it swung round and kept me in front also.

Finally I tried a run straight in but it made another dash for liberty. On three legs, however, it had no chance, and in another minute Jock had it again, and down they came together, rolling over and over once more. The duiker struggled hard, but Jock hung on, and each time it got its feet to the ground to rise he would tug sideways and roll it over again, until I got up to them, and catching the buck by the head, held it down with my knee on its neck and my knife in hand to finish it.

There was, however, still another lesson for us both to learn that day. Neither of us knew what a buck can do with its hind feet when it is down. The duiker was flat on its side. Jock, thinking the fight was over, had let go, and, before I could move the supple body doubled up, and the feet whizzed viciously at me right over its head. Missing my arm, the hoof struck full on the handle of the knife and sent it flying metres out of reach. Faster than the eye could follow them the little feet whizzed and the legs seemed to buzz round like the spokes of a wheel. Holding the horns at arm's length in order to dodge the kicks, I tried to pull the duiker towards the knife, but it was too much for me, and with a sudden twist and a wrench it freed itself and was off again.

All the time Jock was moving round and round panting and licking his chops, stepping in and stepping back, longing to be at it again, but not daring to join in without permission. When the duiker broke away, however, he waited for nothing, and was on to it in one spring. This time he let go as it fell, and jumping free of it, had it by the throat before it could rise. I ran to them again, but the picking up of the knife had delayed me and I was not in time to save Jock the same lesson that the duiker had just taught me.

Down on its side, with Jock's jaws locked in its throat once more, the duiker doubled up and used its feet. The first kick went over his head and scraped harmlessly along his back, but the second caught him at the point of the shoulder, and the razor-like toe ripped his side right to the hip.

Then the dog showed his pluck and cleverness. His side was cut open as if it had been slashed by a knife, but he never flinched or loosened his grip for a second. He seemed to go at it more furiously than ever, but more cleverly and warily. He swung his body round clear of the whizzing feet and tugged away incessantly and vigorously, keeping the buck's neck stretched out and pulling it round in a circle backwards so that it could not possibly double its body up enough to kick him again. Before I could catch the feet to help him, the kicks grew weaker, the buck slackened out, and Jock had won.

The sun was hot, the sand was deep, and the rifle was hard to find. It was a long way back to the wagons, and the duiker made a heavy load. But the end of that first chase seemed so good that nothing else mattered. The only thing I did mind was the open cut on Jock's side. He minded nothing. His tail was going like a telegraph needle, he was panting with his mouth open from ear to ear, and his red tongue was hanging out and making great slapping licks at his chops. He was not still for a second, but kept walking in a circle round the duiker, and looking up at me and then down at it, as if he was not at all sure as to whether it would not be a good thing to have another go in and make it all safe.

He was just as happy as a dog could be, and perhaps he was proud of the wound that left a straight line from his shoulder to his hip, and showed up like a cord under the golden brindle as long as he lived — a memento of his first real hunt.

In the Heart of the Bush

When the hen pecked Jock on the nose, she gave him a useful
lesson in the art of finding out what you want to know
without getting into trouble. As he got older, he also learnt
that there are only certain things which concerned him and
which it was necessary for him to know. A hunting dog has to
learn to mind his own business, as well as to understand it.
Some dogs turn sulky or timid or stupid when they are
checked, but an intelligent dog with a stout heart will learn
to leave things alone.

When I took down the rifle from the wagon, Jock would
give a quick look up and with an eager little run towards me
give a whimper of joy, make two or three bounds as if
wanting to stretch his muscles and loosen his joints. He
would shake himself vigorously as though he had just come
out of the water, and with a soft, contented 'Woo-woo-woo',
drop silently into his place at my heels and give his whole
attention to his work.

He was the best of companions, and through the years
that we hunted together I never tired of watching him.
There was always something to learn, something to admire
and something to be grateful for. Very often there was
something to laugh at — in a way in which we laugh only
at those of whom we are fond.

It was the struggle between Jock's intense keenness and

64

his sense of duty that most often raised the laugh. He knew that his place was behind me, but he also knew that nine times out of ten he scented or saw the game long before I knew there was anything near. Naturally he wanted to be in front or at least abreast of me to show me whatever there was to be seen.

He noticed, just as surely and as quickly as any human being could, any change in my manner. Nothing escaped him, for his eyes and ears were on the move the whole time. It was impossible for me to look for more than a few seconds in any one direction, or to stop or even to turn my head to listen, without being caught by him. His bright brown eyes were everlastingly on the watch and on the move.

When we were after game, and he could scent or see it, he would keep a little bit to the side of me so as to have a clear view. When he knew by my manner that I thought there was game near, he kept so close up that he would often bump against my heels as I walked, or run right into my legs if I stopped suddenly. At these times it was impossible to say anything without risk of scaring the game, and I got into the habit of making signs with my hand which he understood quite as well.

Sometimes I would be in the act of aiming when he would press up against me. I used to get angry with him then, but dared not breathe a word. I would lower my head slowly, turn round, and give him a look. He knew quite well what it meant. Down would go his ears instantly, and he would back away from me, drop his stump of a tail, wag it in a feeble deprecating way, and open his mouth into a sort of foolish laugh that was his apology.

It was quite impossible to be angry with him, he was so keen and he meant so well. When he saw me laughing softly

65

at him, he would come up close to me, cock his tail several centimetres higher and wag it a bit faster.

There is a deal of expression in a dog's tail and it will generally tell you what his feelings are. Once when lost in the veld Jock's tail helped me find the way back.

Nearly every one who goes hunting in the bushveld gets lost some time or other — generally in the beginning before he has learnt to notice things.

Many stories have been told of men being lost. Many volumes could be filled with them for the trouble of writing down what any hunter will tell you. But no one who has not seen it can realise how the thing may happen. No one would believe the effect that the terror of being lost, and the demoralisation which it causes, can have on a sane man's senses. If you want to know that a man can persuade himself to believe against the evidence of his senses — even when his very life depends upon his holding to the absolute truth — then you should see a man who is lost in the bush. He knows that he left the road on the north side; he loses his bearings; he does not know how long, how fast, or how far he has walked; yet if he keeps his head he will make due south and must inevitably strike the road. After going for half an hour and seeing nothing familiar, he begins to feel that he is going in the wrong direction; something pulls at him to face right about. Only a few minutes more of this, and he feels sure that he must have crossed the road without noticing it, and therefore that he ought to be going north instead of south, if he hopes ever to strike it again. How, you will ask, can a man imagine it possible to cross a big dusty road 5 to 10 metres wide without seeing it? The idea seems absurd; yet they do really believe it. One of the first illusions that occurs to men when they lose their heads is that they have done this, and it is the cause of scores of cases of 'lost in the bush'. The idea that they may have done it is absurd enough; but stranger still is the fact that they actually do it.

If you cannot understand a man thinking he had done such a thing, what can you say of a man actually doing it? Impossible, quite impossible, you think. Ah! but it is a fact. Many know it for a fact, and I have witnessed it twice myself, once in Mashonaland and once on the Delagoa road. I saw men, tired, haggard and wild-eyed, staring far in front of them, never looking at the ground, pressing on, on, on, and actually cross well-worn wagon roads, coming from hard veld into a sandy wheel-worn track and kicking up a cloud of dust as they passed, and utterly blind to the fact that they were walking across the roads they had been searching for — in one case for ten hours, and in the other for three days. When we called to them they had already crossed and were disappearing again into the bush. In both cases the sound of the human voice and the relief of being 'found' made them collapse. The knees seemed to give way. They could not remain standing.

The man who loses his head is really lost. He cannot think, remember, reason, or understand. The strangest thing of all is that he often cannot even *see* properly — he fails to see the very things that he most wants to see, even when they are as large as life before him. There is only one rule to remember when you have lost your way, don't lose your head. But indeed, that is just the one rule you are unable to observe.

We were out hunting once and among our party there was one who was very nervous. He had been lost once for six or eight hours, and being haunted by the dread of being lost again, his nerve was all gone and he would not go fifty metres without a companion. However, in the excitement of shooting at and galloping after kudu, this dread was forgotten for a moment. He himself could not tell how it happened that he became separated, and no one noticed.

The strip of wood in which I had taken cover was seven or eight kilometres long but at most only three hundred metres wide. Between the stems of the trees I could see our camp and wagons 400 metres away. Ten or twelve shots faintly heard in the distance told me that the others were on to the kudu, and knowing the preference of those animals for the bush I took cover behind a big stump and waited.

For over half an hour, however, nothing came towards me, and believing then that the game had broken off another way, I was about to return to camp when I heard the tapping of galloping feet a long way off. In a few minutes the hard thud and occasional ring on the ground told that it was not the kudu; and soon afterwards I saw a man on horseback. He was leaning eagerly forward and thumping the exhausted horse with his rifle and his heels to keep up its staggering gallop. I looked about quickly to see what it was he was chasing that could have slipped past me unnoticed, but there was nothing. Thinking there had been an accident and he was coming for help, I stepped out into the open and waited for him to come up.

'What's up, sportsman?' I asked, no louder than you would say it across a tennis-court, but the words brought him up, white-faced and terrified, and he half slid, half tumbled off the horse, gasping out, 'I was lost, I was lost!' How he managed to keep within that strip of bush, without once getting into the open where he would have seen the wagons and the smoke of the big camp fire, he would never explain. I turned him round where he stood, and through the trees showed him the white tents of the wagons and the cattle grazing near by, but he was too dazed to understand or explain anything.

Buggins who was with us in the first season was no hunter, but he was a good shot and not a bad fellow. When he got lost there was much laughter, and — to me — a wonderful revelation. He showed us, as in a play, how you can be lost; how you can walk for ever in one little circle, as though drawn to a centre by magnetic force, and how you can miss seeing things in the bush if they do not move.

We had outspanned in a flat covered with close grass about 60 cm high and shady flat-topped thorn trees. The wagons, four in number, were drawn up a few metres off the road, two abreast. The day was hot and still and when breakfast was over we got into the shade of the wagons, some to sleep and others to smoke.

Buggins — that was his pet name — was a passenger returning to England. He was good-natured, unselfish, and credulous; but he had one fault — he talked until our heads buzzed. He used to sleep contentedly in a rumpled tarpaulin all through the night treks and come up fresh as a daisy and full of accumulated chat at the morning outspan, just when we — unless work or sport called for us — were wanting to get some sleep.

That morning, after breakfast Jimmy, who understood Buggins well, told him pleasantly that he could 'sleep, shoot, or shut up.' To shut up was impossible, and to sleep again difficult, even for Buggins; so with a good-natured laugh he took the shot-gun, saying that he 'would potter around a bit and give us a treat.' Well, he did.

We had outspanned on the edge of an open space in the thorn bush, and into this open arena sallied Buggins, gently drawn by the benevolent purpose of giving us a treat. What he hoped to find in the open on that sweltering day only he could tell. We knew that no living thing but lizards would be out of the shade just then.

He had been gone for more than half an hour when we heard a shot, and a few minutes later Jimmy's voice roused us.

'What the dickens is Buggins doing?' he asked in a tone

so puzzled and interested that we all turned to watch that sportsman. According to Jimmy, he had been walking about in an erratic way for some time on the far side of the open ground — going from the one end to the other and then back again. He disappeared for a few minutes into the bush and then reappeared to again manoeuvre in the open in loops and circles, angles and straight lines. Now he was walking about at a smart pace, looking from side to side apparently seaching for somthing. We could see the whole of the arena as clearly as you can see a cricket-field from the railings — for our wagon formed part of the boundary — but we could see nothing to explain Buggins's manoeuvres. Next we saw him face the thorns opposite, raise his gun very deliberately, and fire into the top of the trees.

'Green pigeons', said Jimmy firmly, and we all agreed that Buggins was after specimens for stuffing. But either our guess was wrong or his aim was bad, for after standing dead still for a minute he resumed his vigorous walk. By this time Buggins fairly fascinated us. Making off some few metres in another direction he climbed on to a fair-sized antheap about two metres high, and balancing himself cautiously on this he deliberately fired off both barrels in quick succession. Then the same idea struck us all together, and 'Buggins is lost' came from several — all choking with laughter.

Jimmy got up and stepping out into the open beside the wagon, called, 'Say, Buggins, what in thunder are you doing?'

To see Buggins slide off the antheap and shuffle shame-facedly back to the wagon was a sight never to be forgotten.

I did not want to get lost and be eaten alive, or even look ridiculous, so I began very carefully. I glanced back regularly to see what the track, trees, rocks, or kopjes looked like from the other side. I carefully noted which side of the road I had turned off, and always kept my eye on the sun. But day after day and month after month went by without accident and I got the beginner's complaint, conceit fever. I thought I was not like other chaps who always have doubts and difficulties in finding their way back, but something exceptional with the real instinct in me. So each day I went further and more boldly off the road, and grew more confident and careless.

The very last thing that would have occurred to me on this particular day was that there was any chance of being lost or any need to take note of where we went. The truth is I did not give the matter a thought at all, but went ahead, as one does with the things that are done every day as matters of habit.

71

Lost in the Veld

We were outspanned near some deep shaded water-holes, and at about three o'clock I took my rifle and wandered off in the hope of coming across something for the larder and having some sport during the three hours before the evening trek began.

We had been going along slowly, for half an hour, without seeing more than a little stembuck scurrying away in the distance, when I noticed that Jock was sniffing about in a way that looked like business. He was not sure of anything; that was clear. He kept trying in different directions, moving at a cautious walk for a few metres and then looking about.

There was a slight rustling in the bush ahead of us and then the sound of feet. I made a dash for the chance of a running shot, but it was too late, and all we saw was half a dozen beautiful kudu disappearing among the tree stems.

It was a bad disappointment for that was the first time we had fairly and squarely come upon kudu. However, it was still early and the game had not been scared, but had gone off quietly. So, hoping for another chance we started off at a trot along the fresh spoor.

A big kudu bull stands as high as a bullock, and although they have the small shapely feet of an antelope the spoor is heavy enough to follow at a trot except on stony ground. Perhaps they know this, for they certainly prefer the rough hard ground when they can get it.

We went along at a good pace, but with many short breaks to make sure of the spoor in the stony parts. It was pretty hot work, although we wore light clothing. A rough flannel shirt, open at the throat, and moleskin trousers dyed with coffee — for khaki was unknown to us then — was the usual wear. We carried as little as possible. Generally a water-bottle filled with unsweetened cold tea and a cartridge belt were all we took besides the rifle. This time I had less than usual. Meaning to be out for a couple of hours at most and to stick close to the road, I had pocketed half a dozen cartridges and left both bandolier and water-bottle behind.

It was not long before we came upon kudu again, but they were on the watch. They were standing in the fringe of some thick bush, broadside on but looking back full at us, and as soon as I stopped to aim the whole lot disappeared with the same easy movement, just melting away in the bush.

If I had only known it. It was a hopeless chase for an inexperienced hunter. They were simply playing with me. The very things that seemed so encouraging to me would have warned an old hand that running on the trail was quite useless. When they moved off quietly, it was not because they did not realise the danger. When they allowed us to catch up to them time after time, it was not because they did not expect us. It was all part of the game. They were keeping in touch with us so that we could not surprise them, and whenever they stopped it was always where they could see us coming through the thinner bush for a long way and where they themselves could disappear in the thick bush in a couple of strides.

The chase was long and tiring, but there was no feeling of disappointment and no thought of giving it up. Each time they came into sight we got keener and more excited, and the end seemed nearer and more certain. I knew that there were six animals; four cows, one young bull, and a magnificent old bull with a glorious head and great spiral horns. I carried his picture in my eye and could pick him out

73

instantly wherever he stood and however motionless; for, incredibly difficult as it is to pick out still objects in the bush before your eye becomes accustomed to it, it is wonderful what you can do when your eye is in and you are cool and intent and know what you are looking for. I had the old bull marked down as mine, and knew his every detail: his splendid bearing, strong shaggy neck with mane to the withers and bearded throat, the soft grey dove-colour of the coat with its white stripes, the easy balancing movement in carrying the massive horns as he cantered away, and the trick of throwing them back to glide them through the bush.

The last run was a long and hard one. The kudu seemed to have taken matters seriously and made up their minds to put a safe distance between us and them. The spooring was often difficult and the pace hot, but we plodded away — the picture of the kudu bull luring me on, and Jock content with any chase.

Without him the spoor would have been lost long before. It was in many places too faint and scattered for me to follow, but he would sniff about quietly, and, by his contented looks back at me, and brisk wagging of that stumpy tail, show that he was on it again. But at last even his help was not enough. We had come to the end of the chase, and not a spoor, scratch, or sign of any sort was to be seen.

Time had passed unnoticed, and it was only when it became clear that further search would be quite useless that I looked at my watch and found it was nearly five o'clock. That was rather a shock, for it seemed reasonable to think that, as we had been out for pretty nearly two hours and going fast for most of the time, it would take almost as long to get back again.

I had not once noticed our direction or looked at the sun, yet when it came to making for camp again the idea of losing the way never occurred to me. I had not the slightest doubt about the way we had come, and it seemed the natural thing to go back the same way.

A short distance from where we finally gave up the chase there was a rise crowned by some good-sized rocks and bare of trees. It was not high enough to be fairly called a kopje, but I climbed it on the chance of getting a view of the surrounding country. The rise was not sufficient, however, to give a view. There was nothing to be seen, and I sat down on the highest rock to rest for a few minutes and smoke a cigarette.

It is over twenty years since that day, but that cigarette is not forgotten, and the little rise where we rested is still, to me, Cigarette Kopje. I was so thoroughly wet from the heat and hard work that the matches in the breast pocket of my shirt were all damp, and the heads came off most of them before one was gently coaxed into giving a light. Five minutes' rest was enough. We both wanted a drink, but there was no time to hunt for water in such a dry part as that, so off we started for camp and jogged along for a good time, perhaps half an hour.

75

Little by little I began to feel some uncertainty about the way and to look about from side to side for reminders. I forgot all about those long stretches in which nothing had been noticed except the kudu spoor, and was unconsciously looking out for things in regular succession which we had passed at quite long intervals. Of course, they were not to be found, but I kept on looking out for them — first feeling annoyed, then puzzled, then worried. Something had gone wrong, and we were not going back on our old tracks.

At the first puzzled stop I tried to recall some of the more noticeable things we had passed during the chase. There were two flat-topped mimosas, looking like great rustic tables on a lawn, and we had passed between them. There was a large antheap, with a twisty top like a crooked mud chimney, behind which the kudu bull had calmly stood watching us approach. Then a marula tree with a fork like a giant catapult stick; and so on with a score of other things, all coming readily to mind.

That was what put me hopelessly wrong. I began to look for particular objects instead of taking one direction and keeping to it. Whenever a flat-topped thorn, a quaint antheap, a patch of tambookie grass, or a forked marula came in sight, I would turn off to see if they were the same we had passed coming out. It was hopeless folly, of course, for in that country there were hundreds and thousands of such things all looking very much alike, and you could walk yourself to death zigzagging about from one to another and never get any nearer home. When it comes to doing that sort of thing your judgement is gone and you have lost your head, and the worst of it is you do not know it and would not believe it if anyone could tell you so. I did not know it, but it was nevertheless the fact.

As the sun sank lower I hurried on faster, but never long in one line — always turning this way and that to search for the particular marks I had in mind. At last we came to four trees in a line, and my heart gave a great jump, for these we had certainly passed before. In order to make quite sure I hunted for kudu spoor. There was none to be seen, but on an old molehill there was the single print of a dog's foot.

'Ha, Jock's!' I exclaimed aloud, and Jock himself at

the sound of his name stepped up briskly and sniffed at his own spoor. Close behind it there was a clear mark of a heeled boot, and there were others further on. There was no doubt about it, they were Jock's and mine, and I could have given a whoop of delight. But a chilly feeling came over me when I realised that the footprints were *leading the same way as we were going*, instead of the opposite way. What on earth did it mean?

I laid the rifle down and sat on an old stump to think it out, and after puzzling over it for some minutes came to the conclusion that by some stupid blunder I must have turned round somewhere and followed the line of the kudu, instead of going back on it. The only thing to be done was to right about face and go faster than ever. Bad as the disappointment was, it was a certain consolation to know that we were on the track at last. That at any rate was a certainty; for, besides the footprints, the general appearance of the country and many individual features were perfectly familiar, now that I took a good look at them from this point.

At that moment I had not a shadow of doubt about the way — no more, indeed, than if we had been on the road itself. No suspicion of the truth occurred to me, yet the simple fact is we were not then on the kudu trail at all, but, having made a complete circle, had come on to our own trail at the molehill and were now doing the circle the second time — but the reverse way now.

The map on the opposite page is an attempt to show what happened. The details are of course only guesswork, but the general idea is correct. The kudu themselves had moved in a rough circle and in the first attempt to return to the wagons I had started back on their trail but must have turned aside somewhere, and after that, by dodging about looking for special landmarks, must have made a complete circle. Thus we eventually came back to the track on which we had started for home, and the things that then looked so convincingly familiar were things seen during the first attempt to return, and not, as I supposed, landmarks on the original kudu trail. Jock's footprints in the molehill were only a few hundred metres from the Cigarette Kopje and about the same distance from where we had lost the kudu spoor. We were at that moment, actually within two kilometres of the wagons.

It seems incredible that one could be so near and not see or understand. Why should one walk in circles instead of taking a fairly straight line? How was it possible to pass Cigarette Kopje and not recognise it? I must have gone within fifty metres or less of it. The answer is that the bush does not allow you to see much. The wagons, for instance, might as well have been 100 kilometres away. As for Cigarette Kopje — things do not look the same unless seen from the same point.

I had passed Cigarette Kopje, it's true. But when coming towards it from a new side it must have looked quite different, and besides that, I had not been expecting it, not looking for it, not even thinking of it — had indeed said goodbye to it for ever. When we turned back at the molehill, beginning to do the circle for the second time, we must have passed quite close to Cigarette Kopje again, but again it was from a different opening in the bush, and this time I had thought of nothing and seen nothing except the things I picked out and recognised as we hurried along. To my half-opened beginner's eyes these things were familiar. We had passed

MAP OF 'LOST IN THE VELD'

Thick black line shows track of kudu.
Thin black line shows first circle beginning Cigarette Kopje and ending at Z, Jocks footprint in molehill!
Dotted line shows second circle from Z, where I turned back again, to Cigarette Kopje.
Arrows show the direction in which we went on each trail.

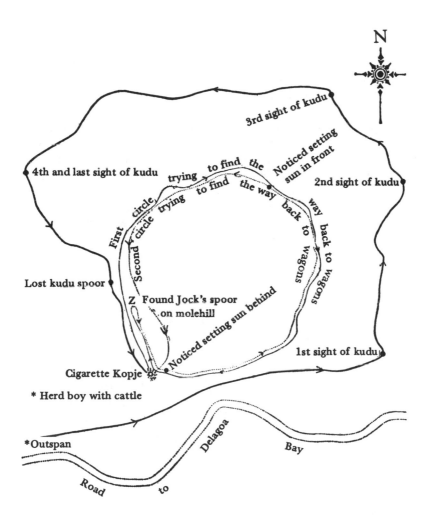

them before; that seemed to be good enough. So, on we went, simply doing the same circle a second time, but this time the reverse way.

The length of my shadow stretching out before me as we started from the molehill was a reminder of the need for haste, and we set off at a smart double. A glance back every few minutes to make sure that we were returning the way we had come was enough, and on we sped, confident that we were securely on the line of the kudu and going straight for the wagons.

It is very difficult to say how long this lasted before once more a horrible doubt arose. It was when we had done half the circle that I was pulled up as if struck in the face. The setting sun shining into my eyes as we crossed an open space stopped me. I remembered that it was my long shadow in front of me as we started from the molehill that had urged me to hurry on. We had started due east. We were going dead west. What on earth was wrong?

I went on, no longer trotting and full of hope but walking heavily and weighted with doubt. The feeling of uncertainty grew until I really did not know whether the familiar-looking objects and scenes were indeed old acquaintances or merely imagination playing tricks in a country where every style and sample was copied a thousand times over.

A few minutes later I again caught sight of the sunset glow — it was on my direct right. This meant that the trail had taken another turn, while I could have sworn we were holding a course straight as an arrow. It was all a hopeless tangle. I was lost then — and knew it.

It was not the dread of a night out in the bush — for after many months of roughing it, that had no great terrors for me — but the helpless feeling of being lost and the anxiety and uncertainty about finding the road again, that gnawed at me and made me feel tucked-up and drawn. I wondered when they would begin to look for me, if they would light big fires and fire shots, and if it would be possible to see or hear the signals. The light would not last much longer. The dimness, the silence, and the hateful doubts about the trail made it more and more difficult to recognise the line. So, I thought it was time to fire a signal shot.

There was no answer. It was silly to hope for one. For even if it had been heard they would only have thought that I was shooting at something. Yet the clinging to hope was so strong that every twenty metres or so I stopped to listen for a reply; and when, after what seemed an eternity, none came, I fired another.

When you shoot in the excitement of the chase the noise of the report does not strike you as anything out of the way, but a signal shot when you are alone and lost seems to fill the world with sound and to shake the earth itself. It has a most chilling effect, and the feeling of loneliness becomes acute as the echoes die away and still no answer comes.

Another short spell of tip-toe walking and intent listening, and then it came to me that one shot as a signal was useless. I should have fired more and at regular intervals, like minute-guns at sea. I felt in my pocket: there were only four cartridges there and one in the rifle. There was night before me, with the wolves and the lions; there was the food for tomorrow, and perhaps more than tomorrow. There could be no minute-guns: two shots were all that could be spared, and I looked about for some high and open ground where the sound would travel far and wide.

Ahead of us to the right the trees seemed fewer and the light stronger. There I came upon some rising ground bare of bush. It was not much for my purpose, but it was higher than the rest and quite open, and there were some rocks scattered about the top. The same old feeling of mixed remembrance and doubt came over me as we climbed it: it looked familiar and yet different. Was it memory or imagination?

But there was no time for wonderings. From the biggest rock, which was only waist high, I fired off two of my precious cartridges, and stood like a statue listening for the reply. The silence seemed worse than before. The birds had gone to roost, even the flies had disappeared. There was no sound at all but the beat of my own heart and Jock's panting breath.

There were three cartridges and a few damp matches left. There was no sun to dry them now, but I laid them

out carefully on the smooth warm rock, and hoped that one at least would serve to light our camp fire. There was no time to waste. While the light lasted I had to drag up wood for the fire and pick a place for the camp — somewhere where the rocks behind and the fire in front would shelter us from the lions and hyenas, and where I could watch and listen for signals in the night.

There was plenty of wood near by, and thinking anxiously of the damp matches I looked about for dry tindery grass so that any spark would give a start for the fire. As I stooped to look for the grass I came on a patch of bare ground between the scattered tufts, and in the middle of it there lay a half-burnt match. Such a flood of relief and hope surged up that my heart beat up in my throat. Where there were matches there had been men. We were not in the wilds, then, not off the beaten track, perhaps not far from the road itself.

You must experience it to know what it meant at that moment. It drew me on to look for more. A metre away I found the burnt end of a cigarette; and before there was time to realise why that should seem queer, I came on eight or ten matches with their heads knocked off.

For a moment things seemed to go round and round. I sat down with my back against the rock and a funny choky feeling in my throat. I knew they were my matches and cigarette, and that we were exactly where we had started from hours before, when we gave up the chase of the kudu. I began to understand things then. Why places and landmarks seemed familiar; why Jock's spoor in the molehill had pointed the wrong way; why my shadow was in front and behind and beside me in turns. We had been going round in a circle. I jumped up and looked about me with a fresh light; and it was all clear as noonday then. Why, this was the fourth time we had been on or close to some part of this same rise that day. It was the second time I had sat on that very rock. And there was nothing odd or remarkable about that either, for each time I had been looking for the highest point to spy from and had naturally picked the rock-topped rise. I had not recognised it, only because we came upon it from different sides each time and I was thinking of other things all the while.

All at once it seemed as if my eyes were opened and all was clear at last. I knew what to do. Just make the best of it for the night; listen for shots and watch for fires. If by morning no help came in that way, then strike a line due south for the road and follow it up until we found the wagons. It might take all day or even more, but we were sure of water that way and one could do it. The relief of really understanding was so great that the thought of a night out no longer worried me.

There was enough wood gathered, and I stretched out on the grass to rest as there was nothing else to do. We were both tired out, hot, dusty, and very very thirsty; but it was too late to hunt for water. I was lying on my side chewing a grass stem, and Jock lay down in front of me about a metre away. It was a habit of his. He liked to watch my face, and often when I rolled over to ease one side and lie on the other he would get up and come round deliberately to the other side and sling himself down in front of me again. There he would lie with his hind legs sprawled on one side, his front legs straight out, and his head resting on his paws. He would lie like that without a move, his little dark eyes fixed on mine and he would blink and blink, like a drowsy child, fighting against sleep until it beat him.

In the loneliness of that evening I looked into his bright faithful eyes, so soft and brown when there was nothing to do, but so beady black when it came to fighting. I felt very friendly to the comrade who was little more than a puppy still; and he seemed to feel something too; for as I lay there

chewing the straw and looking at him, he stirred his stump of
a tail in the dust a couple of centimetres from time to time to
let me know that he understood all about it and that it was
all right as long as we were together.

But an interruption came. Jock suddenly switched up
his head, put it a bit sideways as a man would do, and listened
over his shoulder with his nose up in the air. I watched him,
and thinking that it was probably only a buck out to feed in
the cool of the evening, I tickled his nose with the long straw,
saying, 'No good, old chap; only three cartridges left. We
must keep them.'

Jock got up and, as if to show me that I was frivolous
and not attending properly to business, turned away from
me and with his ears cocked began to listen again.

He was standing slightly in front of me and I happened
to notice his tail. It was drooping slightly and perfectly
still. He kept it like that as he stepped quietly forward on
to another sloping rock overlooking a side where we had
not yet been. Evidently there was something there, but he
did not know what, and he wanted to find out.

I watched him, much amused by his calm business-like
manner. He walked to the edge of the rock and looked
out. For a few minutes he stood stock-still with his ears
cocked and his tail motionless; then his ears dropped and
his tail wagged gently from side to side.

Something that I had never quite known before — an
instinct or sympathy quickened by the day's experience —
taught me to understand, and I jumped up, thinking, 'He sees
something that he knows. He is pleased.'

As I walked over to him, he looked back at me with his mouth open and tongue out, his ears still down and his tail wagging — he was smiling all over, in his own way. I looked out over his head, and there, about three hundred metres off, were the oxen peacefully grazing, and the herd-boy in his red coat lounging along behind them.

Shame at losing myself and dread of the others' chaff kept me very quiet, and all they knew for many months was that we had had a long fruitless chase after kudu and hard work to get back in time.

I had had my lesson, and did not require to have it rubbed in and be roasted as Buggins had been. Only Jock and I knew all about it. But once or twice there were anxious nervous moments when it looked as if we were not the only ones in the secret. The big Zulu driver, Jim Makokel' — always interested in hunting and all that concerned Jock — asked me as we were inspanning at what I had fired the last two shots. I pretended not to hear or to notice the question, and he went on to say how he had told the other drivers that it must have been a klipspringer on a high rock or a monkey or a bird because the bullets had whistled over the wagons. I told him to inspan and not talk so much, and moved round to the other side of the wagon.

That night I slept hard, but woke up once dreaming that several lions were looking down at me from the top of a big flat rock and Jock was keeping them off.

Jock was in his usual place beside me, lying against my blankets. I gave him an extra pat for the dream, thinking, 'Good old boy; we know all about it, you and I, and we're not going to tell. But we've learned some things that we won't forget.' And as I dropped off to sleep again I felt a few feeble sleepy pats against my leg, and knew it was Jock's tail wagging 'Good-night'.

The Impala Stampede

Not all our days were spent in excitement — far far from it. For six or seven months the rains were too heavy, the heat too great, the grass too rank, and the fever too bad in the bushveld for any one to do any good there. So that for more than half of the year we had no hunting to speak of. Even during the hunting season there were many off-days and long spells when we never fired a shot. The work with the wagons was hard when we had full loads. The trekking was slow and at night, so that there was always something to do in the daytime — repairs to be done, oxen to be doctored, grass and water to be looked for, and so on; and we had to make up sleep when we could.

Even when the sport was good and the bag satisfactory there was usually nothing new to tell about it. So Jock and I had many a long spell when there was no hunting, many a bad day when we worked hard but had no sport, and many a good day when we got what we were after, and nothing happened that would interest any one else.

Every hunt was exciting and interesting for us, even those in which we got nothing. To tell all that happened would be to tell the same old story many times over; but indeed, it would not be possible to tell all, for there were some things — the most interesting of all, perhaps — which only Jock knew.

He had a few hard chases after animals which I thought were wounded but were not hit at all until he realised that he was a better judge than his master. He went off the instant he was sent, but if there was nothing wounded — that is, if he could not pick up a 'blood spoor' — he would soon show it by casting across the trail, instead of following hard on it.

Often he would come back of his own accord, and there was something quite peculiar in his look when he returned from these wild-goose chases. I got to know that look quite well. To me it meant, 'Well, that job was a failure — finished and done for. Now is there anything else you can think of?'

What always seemed to me so curious and full of meaning was that he never once looked back in the direction of the unwounded game, but seemed to put them out of his mind altogether as of no further interest. It was very different when he got on to the trail of a wounded buck and I had to call him off, as was sometimes necessary when the chase looked hopeless or it was too late to go further. He would obey, of course — no amount of excitement made him forget that; but he would follow me in a sort of sideways trot, looking back over his shoulder all the time.

Twice I thought he was lost for ever through following wounded game. The first occasion was also the first time that we got among the impala and saw them in numbers. There is no more beautiful and fascinating sight than that of a troop of impala or springbuck really on the move and jumping in earnest. The height and distance that they clear is simply incredible. The impala's greater size and its delicate spiral horns give it a special distinction; the springbuck's brilliant white and red, and the divided crest which fans out along the spine when it is excited, are unique. But who can say which of the many beautiful antelopes is the most beautiful? The oldest hunter will tell you of first one, then another, and then another, as they come to mind, just as he saw them in some supreme unforgettable moment; and each at that moment has seemed quite the most beautiful animal in the world.

It is when they are jumping that the impala are seen at their best.

Every hunter has seen a whole troop clear a road or

donga six metres wide, apparently in an effortless stride. You stand and watch in speechless admiration. The gasp at the first glorious leap is followed by steady silent wonder at the regularity of the numbers.

Then suddenly you see one animal take off away back behind the others, shoot up, and sail high above the arch of all the rest, and with head erect and feet comfortably gathered, land far beyond them. The difference between ease and effort, the perfect grace of both. Something is wrung from you — a word, a gasp — and you stand breathless with wonder and admiration until the last one is gone. You have forgotten to shoot, but they have left you something better than a trophy, something which time only will glorify — a picture that in daylight or in dark will fill your mind whenever you hear the name Impala.

Something of this I carried away from my first experience among them.

We had gone out after breakfast, striking well away from the main road until we got among the thicker thorns where there was any amount of fresh spoor and we were quite certain to find a troop sooner or later. Several times I heard sounds of rustling bush or feet cantering away. Something had heard us and made off unseen. I dropped down into the sandy bed of a dry donga and used it as a stalking trench. From this it was easy enough to have a good look around every hundred metres or so without risk of being heard or seen.

We had been going along cautiously in this way for some time when, peering over the bank, I spied a single impala half hidden by a scraggy bush. It seemed queer that there should be only one, as their habit is to move in troops, but there was nothing else to be seen. Indeed it was only the flicker of an ear on this one that had caught my eye. Nothing else in the land moved.

Jock climbed the bank also, following so closely that he bumped against my heels, and when I lay flat actually crawled over my legs to get up beside me and see what was on. Little by little he got into the way of imitating all I did, so that after a while it was hardly necessary to say a word or make a sign to him. He lay down beside me and

88

raised his head to look just as he saw me do. He was all
excitement, trembling like a wet spaniel on a cold day, and
instead of looking steadily at the impala as I was doing
and as he usually did, he was looking here, there and everywhere. It seemed almost as if he was looking at things — not
for them. It was my comfortable belief at the moment that
he had not yet spotted the buck, but was looking about
anxiously to find out what was interesting me. It turned out,
as usual, that he had seen a great deal more than his master
had.

The stalking looked very easy, as a few metres further
up the donga there was excellent cover in some dense thorns,
behind which we could walk boldly across open ground to
within easy range of the buck and get a clear shot. We reached
the cover all right, but I had not taken three steps into the
open space beyond before there was a rushing and scrambling
on every side of me. The place was a whirlpool of racing and
plunging impala. They came from every side and went in
every direction as though caught suddenly in an enclosure
and, mad with fear and bewilderment, were trying to find a
way out. How many there were it was quite impossible to
say. The bush was alive with them, and the dust they kicked
up, the noise of their feet, their curious sneezy snorts, and
their wild confusion completely bewildered me. Not one
stood still. Never for a moment could I see any single animal
clearly enough or long enough to fire at it. They seemed to
me to whirl like leaves in a wind eddy. My eyes could not
follow them and my brain swam as I looked.

It was a hot day. There was no breeze at all, and the

herd had probably been resting after their morning feed and drink when we came upon them. By creeping up along the donga we had managed to get unobserved right into the middle of the dozing herd, so they were literally on every side of us. At times it looked as if they were bound to stampede over us and simply trample us down, for in their panic they saw nothing, and not one appeared to know what or where the danger was. Time and again, as for part of a second I singled one out and tried to aim, others would come racing straight for us, compelling me to switch round to face them, only to find them swerve with a dart or a mighty bound when within a few paces of me.

What Jock was doing during that time I do not know. It was all such a whirl of excitement and confusion that there are only a few clear impressions left on my mind. One is of a buck coming through the air right at me, jumping over the backs of two others racing across my front. I can see now the sudden wriggle of its body and the look of terror in its eyes when it saw me and realised that it was going to land almost at my feet. I tried to jump aside, but it was not necessary: with one touch on the ground it shot slantingly past me like a ricochet bullet. Another picture that always comes back is that of a splendid ram clearing the first of the dense thorn bushes that were to have been my cover in stalking. He flew over it outlined against the sky in the easiest most graceful and most perfect curve imaginable. It came back to me afterwards that he was eight or ten metres from me, and yet I had to look up into the sky to see his white chest and gracefully gathered feet as he cleared the thorn bush like a soaring bird.

One shot, out of three or four fired in desperation as they were melting away, hit something; the unmistakable thud of the bullet told me so. The wounded animal went off with the rest and I followed, with Jock ahead of me hot on the trail.

A hundred metres further on, where Jock with his nose to the ground had raced along between some low stones and a marula tree, I came to a stop — bush all round me, not a living thing in sight, and all as silent as the grave. On one of the smooth hot stones there were smears on the long yellow grass, and it was clear enough, judging by the height of the

90

blood-marks from the ground, that the impala was wounded in the body — probably far back, as there were no frothy bubbles to show a lung shot.

I knew that it would be a long chase unless Jock could head the buck off and bay it. However, unless he did this at once, there was little chance of my finding him. The trail became more and more difficult to follow. The blood was less frequent, and the hot sun dried it so quickly that it was more than I could do to pick it out from the red streaks on the grass and many coloured leaves. So I gave it up and sat down to smoke and wait.

Half an hour passed, and still no Jock. Then I wandered about, whistling and calling for him. Calling until the sound of my own voice became quite uncanny, the only sound in an immense silence.

Two hours passed in useless calling and listening, searching and waiting, and then I gave it up altogether and made back for the wagons, trying to hope against my real conviction that Jock had struck the road somewhere and had followed it to the outspan, instead of coming back on his own trail through the bush to me.

But there was no Jock at the wagons. My heart sank, although I was not surprised. It was nearly four hours since he had disappeared, and it was as sure as anything could be that something extraordinary must have happened or he would have come back to me long before this. No one at the wagons had seen him since we started out together; and there was nothing to be done but to wait and see what would happen. It was perfectly useless to look for him. If he was alive and well, he was better able to find his way than the best tracker that ever lived; if he was dead, or injured and unable to move, there was not one chance in a million of finding him.

The big Zulu wagon driver, Jim Makokel', took a real pride in Jock which began the day Jock fought the table-

leg and grew stronger and stronger to the end. Jim became Jock's devoted champion, and more than once, as will be seen, showed that he would face man or beast to stand by him when he needed help.

This day when I returned to the wagons Jim was sitting with the other drivers in the group round the big pot of porridge. I saw him give one quick look my way and heard him say sharply to the others, 'Where is the dog? Where is Jock?' He stood there looking at me with a big wooden spoon full of porridge stopped on the way to his mouth. In a few minutes they all knew what had happened. The other drivers took it calmly, saying composedly that the dog would find his way back. But Jim was not calm. It was not his nature. At one moment he would agree with them, swamping them with a flood of reasons why Jock, the best dog in the world, would be sure to come back; and the next — hot with restless excitement — would picture all that the dog might have been doing and all that he might still have to face, and then break off to proclaim loudly that every one ought to go out and hunt for him. Jim was not practical or reasonable — he was too excitable for that, but he was very loyal, and it was his way to show his feelings by doing something — generally and preferably by fighting someone. Knowing only too well how uscless it would be to search for Jock, I lay down under the wagon to rest and wait.

After half an hour of this Jim could restrain himself no longer. He came over to where I lay, and with a look of severe disapproval and barely controlled indignation, asked me for a gun, saying that he himself meant to go out and look for Jock. It would be nearer the mark to say that he demanded a gun. He was so genuinely anxious and so indignant at what he considered my indifference that it was impossible to be angry; and I let him talk away to me and at me in his exciting bullying way. He would take no answer and listen to no reason. So, finally to keep him quiet I gave him the shot-gun, and off he went, muttering his opinions of every one else — a great springy striding picture of fierce resolution.

He came back nearly three hours later, silent, morose, hot and dusty. He put the gun down beside me without a word —

just a click of disgust. As he strode across to his wagon he called roughly to one of the drivers for the drinking water. Lifting the bucket to his mouth he drank like an ox and slammed it down again without a word of thanks; then sat down in the shade of the wagon, filled his pipe, and smoked in silence.

The trekking hour came and passed, but we did not move. The sun went down, and in the quiet of the evening we heard the first jackals yapping — the first warning of the night. There were still lions and leopards in those parts, and any number of hyenas and wild dogs, and the darker it grew and the more I thought of it, the more hopeless seemed Jock's chance of getting through a night in the bush trying to work his way back to the wagons.

It was almost dark when I was startled by a yell from Jim Makokel', and looking round, saw him bound out into the road shouting, 'He has come, he has come! What did I tell you?' He ran out to Jock, stooping to pat and talk to him, and then in a lower voice and with growing excitement went on rapidly, 'See the blood! See it! He has fought. He has killed! Dog of all dogs! Jock, Jock!' and his savage song of triumph broke off in a burst of rough tenderness, and he called the dog's name five or six times with every note of affection and welcome in his deep voice.

Jock took no notice of Jim's dancing out to meet him, nor of his shouts, endearments and antics. Slowing his tired trot down to a walk, he came straight on to me, flickered his ears a bit, wagged his tail cordially, and gave my hand a splashy lick as I patted him. Then he turned round in the direction he had just come from, looked steadily out, cocked his ears well up, and moved his tail slowly from side to side. For the next half-hour or so he kept repeating this action every few minutes. Even without that I knew that it had been no wild-goose chase, and that kilometres away in the bush there was something lying dead which he could show me if I would but follow him back again to see.

What had happened in the eight hours since he had dashed off in pursuit can only be guessed. That he had pulled down the impala and killed it seemed certain — and what a chase and what a fight it must have been to take all that time. What

93

a fight it must have been to kill an animal six or eight times his own weight and armed with such horns and hoofs. But was it only the impala? Or had the hyenas and wild dogs followed up the trail, as they so often do, and did Jock have to fight his way through them too?

He was hollow-flanked and empty, parched with thirst, and so blown that his breath still caught in suffocating chokes. He was covered with blood and sand. He was a little lame in one fore-leg, but there was no cut or swelling to show the cause. There was only one mark to be seen: over his right eye there was a bluish line where the hair had been shaved off clean, leaving the skin smooth and unbroken. What did it? Was it horn, hoof, tooth, or — what? Only Jock knew.

Hovering round and over me, pacing backwards and forwards between the wagons like a caged animal, Jim, growing more and more excited, filled the air with his talk, his shouts and savage song.

I called for water. 'Water!' roared Jim, 'bring water.' Glaring round he made a spring — stick in hand — at the nearest driver. The man fled in terror, with Jim after him and brought a bucket of water. Jim snatched it from him and sent him sprawling on the ground. Jock took the water in great gulpy bites broken by pauses to get his breath again; and Jim paced up and down — talking, talking, talking. Talking to me, to the others, to Jock, to the world at large, to the heavens, and to the dead. He told of all Jock had done and might have done and would yet do; comparing him with the fighting heroes of his own race, and wandering off into vivid recitals of single episodes and great battles. Time after time I called him, and tried to quiet him; but he was beyond control.

The night closed in. The flames of the camp fires died down, and Jock lay sleeping, but even in his sleep came little spells of panting, like the after-sobs of a child that has cried itself to sleep. We lay rolled in our blankets, and no sound came from where the drivers slept.

But Jim sat on his rough three-legged stool, elbows on knees and hands clasped together, staring intently into the coals. The fit worked slowly off, and his excitement died gradually away. Slowly but surely he subsided until at last there were only occasional mutterings of 'Ow, Jock!' followed by the Zulu click, the expressive shake of the head, and that appreciative half grunt, half chuckle by which they pay tribute to what seems truly wonderful. He wanted no sleep that night. He sat on, waiting for the morning trek, staring into the red coals, and thinking of the bygone glories of his race in the days of the mighty Chaka.

That was Jim, when the fit was on him — transported by some trifling and unforeseen incident from the humdrum of the road, to the life he once had lived with splendid recklessness.

95

Jock's Night Out

Jock was lost twice. It came about both times through his following up wounded animals and leaving me behind, in the days when our hunting was all done on foot. When I could afford a horse and could keep pace with him that difficulty did not trouble us.

The experience with the impala had made me very careful not to let him go unless I felt sure that the game was hard hit and that he would be able to pull it down or bay it. But it is not always easy to judge that. A broken leg shows at once, but a body shot is very difficult to place. Animals shot through the lungs, and even through the lower part of the heart, often go away at a cracking pace and are out of sight in no time, perhaps to keep it up for kilometres, perhaps to drop dead within a few minutes.

After that day with the impala we had many good days together and many hard ones. We had our disappointments, but we had our triumphs, and we were both getting to know our way about by degrees. Buck of many kinds had fallen to us, but so far as I was concerned there was one disappointment that was not to be forgotten. The picture of that kudu bull as he appeared for the last time looking over the antheap the day we were lost was always before me. Like other kinds of game, kudu were not to be found everywhere. They favoured some localities more than others, and when we passed through their known haunts chances of smaller game were often neglected in the hope of coming across the kudu.

One afternoon the herdsman came in to say that there was a stembuck feeding among the oxen only a couple of hundred metres away. He had been quite close to it, he said, and it was very tame. This bonny little red-brown fellow was not a bit scared. From time to time he turned his head our way and, with his large shapely sensitive ears thrown forward, examined us frankly while he moved slightly one way or another so as to keep under cover of the oxen and continue his browsing.

In and out among some seventy head of cattle we played hide-and-seek for quite a while — I not daring to fire for fear of hitting one of the bullocks — until at last he found himself manoeuvred out of the troop. Without giving me a chance, he was off into the bush in a few frisky skips. I followed quietly, knowing that as he was on the feed and not scared, he would not go far.

Moving along silently under good cover I reached a thick scrubby bush and peered over the top of it to search the grass under the surrounding thorn trees for the little red-brown form. I was looking low down in the russety grass — for he was only about twice the size of Jock, and not easy to spot — when a movement on a higher level caught my eye. It was just the flip of a fly-tickled ear; but it was a movement where all else was still, and instantly the form of a kudu cow appeared before me as a picture is thrown on a screen.

There it stood within fifty metres, the soft grey-and-white looking still softer in the shadow of the thorns, but as clear to me   and as still — as a figure carved in stone. The stem of a mimosa hid the shoulders, but all the rest was plainly visible as it stood there utterly unconscious of danger. The tree made a dead shot almost impossible, but the risk in trying for another position was too great, and I fired. The thud of the bullet and the tremendous bound of the kudu straight up in the air told that the shot had gone home. But these things were for a time forgotten in the surprise that followed.

At the sound of the shot twenty other kudu jumped into life and sight before me. The one I had seen and shot was but one of a herd dozing peacefully in the shade, and strangest of all, it was the one that was furthest from me. To the right and left of this one, at distances from fifteen to thirty metres from me, the magnificent creatures had been standing, and I had not seen them. It was the flicker of this one's ear alone that had caught my eye. My bewil-

97

derment was complete when I saw the big bull of the herd
start off twenty metres on my right front and pass away
like a streak in a few sweeping strides. It was a matter of
seconds only, and they were all out of sight — all except
the wounded one, which had turned off from the others.
For all the flurry and confusion I had not lost sight of her,
and noting her tucked-up appearance and shortened
strides set Jock on her trail, believing that she would be
down in a few minutes.

It is not necessary to go over it all again. It was much
the same as the impala chase. I came back tired, disappointed, beaten, and without Jock. It was only after darkness
set in that things began to look serious. When it came to
midnight, with the camp wrapped in silence and in sleep, and
there was still no sign of Jock, things looked very black
indeed.

I heard his panting breath before it was possible to see
anything. It was past one o'clock when he returned.

As we had missed the night trek to wait for Jock I
decided to stay on where we were until the next evening
and to have another try for the wounded kudu, with the
chance of coming across the troop again.

By daybreak Jock did not seem much the worse for his
night's adventures. He seemed a little stiff, and flinched
when I pressed his sides and muscles, but he was as game as
ever when he saw the rifle taken down.

The kudu had been shot through the body, and even without being run to death by Jock must have died in the night,
or have lain down and become too cold and stiff to move. If

it had not been discovered by wild animals there was a good chance of finding it untouched in the early morning, but after sunrise every minute's delay meant fresh risk from the aasvogels. There is very little which, if left uncovered, will escape their eyes. You may leave your buck for help to bring the meat in, certain from the most careful scrutiny that there is not one of these creatures in sight, and return in half an hour to find nothing but a few bones, the horns and hoofs, a rag of skin, and a group of disgusting gorged vultures squatting on a patch of ground all smeared, torn and feather-strewn from their voracious struggles.

In the winter sky — a dome of spotless polished steel — nothing, you would think, can move unseen. Yet they are there. In the early morning, from their white-splashed eyries on some distant mountain they slide off like a launching ship into their sea of blue, and, striking the currents of the upper air, sweep round and upwards in immense circles, their huge motionless wings carrying them higher and higher until they are lost to human sight.

Lie on your back in some dense shade where no side-lights strike in, but where an opening above forms a sort of natural telescope to the sky, and you may see tiny specks where nothing could be seen before. Take your field-glasses, the specks are vultures circling up on high. Look again, and far, far above you will see still other specks, and for aught you know there may be others still beyond. How high are they? And what can they see from there? Who knows? But this is sure, that within a few minutes scores will come swooping down in great spiral rushes where not one was visible before. My own belief is that they watch each other, tier above tier, away in the limitless heavens — watching jealously, as hungry dogs do, for the least suspicious sign — to swoop down and share the spoil.

In the dewy cool of the morning we soon reached the place where Jock had left me behind the evening before. From there on he led the way. As far as I was concerned, there was nothing to guide me, and it was impossible to know what he was after. Did he understand that it was not fresh game but the wounded kudu that I wanted? And, if so, was he following the scent of the old chase or merely what he

99

might remember of the way he had gone? It seemed impossible that scent could lie in that dry country for twelve hours, yet it was clearly nose more than eyes that guided him. He went ahead soberly and steadily, and once when he stopped completely, to sniff at a particular tuft of grass, I found out what was helping him. The grass was well streaked with dry blood.

Jock was some distance ahead of me, trotting along quietly, when I saw him look up, give that rare growling bark of his — one of suppressed but real fury — lower his head, and charge. Then came heavy flapping and scrambling and the wind of huge wings, as twenty or thirty great lumbering aasvogels flopped along the ground with Jock dashing furiously about among them — taking flying leaps at them as they rose, and his jaws snapping like rat-traps as he missed them.

On a little open flat of hard-baked sand lay the stripped frame of the kudu. The head and leg-bones were missing and meat-stripped fragments were scattered all about. Fifty metres away among some bushes Jock found the head, and still further afield were remains of skin and thigh-bones crushed almost beyond recognition. No aasvogel had done this. It was hyenas' work.

I looked at Jock. The mane on his back and shoulders which had risen at the sight of the vultures was not flat yet. He was sniffing about slowly and carefully on the spoor of the hyenas and wild dogs, and he looked 'fight' all over. But what it all meant was beyond me. I could only guess what had happened out in the silent ghostly bush that night.

The Kudu Bull

It often happens when you come unexpectedly upon game that they are off before you see them, and the only chance you have of getting anything is with a running shot. If they go straight from you the shot is not a very difficult one, and a common result of such a shot is the breaking of one of the hind legs between the hip and the hock. While following a rietbuck which I had wounded in this way, Jock learned a clever trick. He had made several tries at its nose and throat, but the buck was going too strongly and was out of reach. Moreover it would not stop or turn when he headed it, but charged straight on, bounding over him. In trying once more for the throat he cannoned against the buck's shoulder and was sent rolling metres away. This seemed to madden him. Racing up behind he flew at the dangling leg, caught it at the shin, and thrusting his feet well out, simply dragged until the buck slowed down, and then began furiously tugging sideways. The crossing of the legs brought the wounded animal down immediately and Jock had it by the throat before it could rise again.

Everyone who is good at anything has some favourite method or device of his own: that was Jock's. He perfected it

101

and used it whenever it was possible. Only once he made a mistake; and he paid for it — very nearly with his life.

We were in a grove of bushy wild plums and scattered thorn-bushes. I stopped to look out between the bushes on to the more open ground beyond and saw a kudu cow walk quietly up the slope from the water-hole. Before there was time to raise the rifle her easy stride had carried her behind a small mimosa tree. I took one quick step out to follow her up and found myself face to face at less than a dozen metres with a grand kudu bull.

It is impossible to convey in words any real idea of the scene and how things happened. Of course it was only for a fraction of a second that we looked straight into each other's eyes; yet it is the first sight that remains with me. The proud head, the huge spiral horns, and the wide soft staring eyes — before the wildness of panic struck them. The picture seems photographed on eye and brain, never to be forgotten. A whirlwind of dust and leaves marked his course as he turned and fled and through it I fired, unsteadied by excitement and hardly able to see. The right hind leg swung out and the great creature sank for a moment, almost to the ground. The sense of triumph, the longed for and unexpected success, went to my head like a rush of blood.

There had been no time to aim, and the shot — a real snap shot — was not at all a bad one. I fired again as the kudu recovered himself, but he was then seventy or eighty metres away and partly hidden at times by trees and scrub. He struck up the slope, following the line of the troop through the scattered thorns. And there, running hard and dropping quickly to my knee for steadier aim, I fired again and again — but each time a longer shot and more obscured by the intervening bush; and no tell-tale thud came to cheer me on.

Forgetting the last night's experience, forgetting everything except how we had twice chased and twice lost them, seeing only another grand prize slipping away, I sent Jock on and followed as fast as I could.

The old Martini carbine had one bad fault; even I could not deny that. Years of rough and careless treatment in all

sorts of weather — for it was only a discarded old mounted police weapon — had told on it, and both in barrel and breech it was well pitted with rust scars. One result of this was that it was always jamming, and unless the cartridges were kept well greased the empty shells would stick and the ejector fail to work. This was almost sure to happen when the carbine became hot from quick firing. It jammed now, and fearing to lose sight of the chase I dared not stop a second, but ran on, struggling from time to time to wrench the breach open.

Reaching the place where they had disappeared, I saw with intense relief and excitement Jock and the kudu having it out less than a hundred metres away. The kudu's leg was broken right up in the ham, and it was a terrible handicap for an animal so big and heavy, but his nimbleness and quickness were astonishing. It was a fight for life and a grand sight; for the kudu, in spite of his wound, easily held his own. No doubt he had fought out many a life and death struggle to win and hold his place as lord of the herd and knew every trick of attack and defence. Maybe too he was blazing with anger and contempt for this persistent little gadfly that worried him so and kept out of reach.

Sometimes he snorted and feinted to charge. At other

times he backed slowly, giving way to draw the enemy on. Then with a sudden lunge the great horns swished like a scythe covering the spot where Jock had been a fraction of a second before. There were pauses too in which he watched his tormentor steadily, with occasional impatient shakes of the head, or, raising it to full height, towered up, a monument of splendid and contemptuous indifference, looking about with big angry but unfrightened eyes for the herd — his herd — that had deserted him.

Keeping what cover there was I came up slowly behind them, struggling and using all the force I dared, short of smashing the lever, to get the empty cartridge out. At last one of the turns in the fight brought me in view, and the kudu dashed off again. For a little way the pace seemed as great as ever, but it soon died away. The driving power was gone, the strain and weight on the one sound leg and the tripping of the broken one were telling, and from then on I was close enough to see it all. In the first rush the kudu seemed to dash right over Jock. Then I saw Jock looking up at it and making furious jumps for its nose. The kudu holding its nose high and well forward, was out of his reach, however, and galloped heavily on, completely ignoring his attacks.

Perhaps he realised that attack in front was useless, for now Jock went determinedly for the broken leg. It swung about in wild eccentric curves, but at the third or fourth attempt he got it and hung on. With all fours spread he dragged along the ground. The first startled spring of the kudu jerked him into the air, but there was no let go now.

Ineffectual and even hopeless as it looked at first, Jock's attacks soon began to tell. The kudu made wild efforts to get at him, but with every turn he turned too, and did it so vigorously that the staggering animal swayed over and had to plunge violently to recover its balance. So they turned this way and that, until a wilder plunge swung Jock off his feet, throwing the broken leg across the other one. With feet firmly planted, Jock tugged again, and the kudu trying to regain its footing was tripped by the crossed legs and came down with a crash.

As it fell Jock was round and fastened on the nose. But it was no duiker, impala or rietbuck that he had to deal

104

with this time. The kudu gave a snort of indignation and shook its head. It shook Jock, whipping the ground with his swinging body, and with another indignant snort and toss of the head flung him off, sending him skidding along the ground on his back.

The kudu had fallen on the wounded leg and failed to rise with the first effort. Jock, while still slithering along the ground on his back was tearing at the air with his feet in his mad haste to get back to the attack, and as he scrambled up, he raced in again with head down and the little eyes black with fury. He was too mad to be wary, and my heart stood still as the long horns went round with a swish. One black point seemed to pierce him through and through, showing a foot out the other side, and a jerky twist of the great head sent him twirling like a tip-cat two to three metres up in the air. It had just missed him, passing under his stomach next to the hind legs. But, until he dropped with a thud and, tearing and scrambling to his feet, raced in again, I felt certain he had been gored through.

The kudu was up again, and it was a running fight from then on. The instant the kudu turned Jock was on to the leg again, and nothing could shake his hold. I had to keep at a respectful distance, for the bull was still good for a furious charge, even with Jock hanging on, and eyed me in the most unpromising fashion whenever I attempted to head it off or even to come close up.

105

The big eyes were bloodshot, but there was no look of fear in them — they blazed with baffled rage. Impossible as it seemed to shake Jock off or to get away from us, and in spite of the broken leg and loss of blood, the furious attempts to beat us off did not slacken. It was a desperate running fight, and right bravely he fought it to the end.

Partly barring the way in front were the whitened trunks and branches of several trees struck down by some storm of the year before, and running ahead of the kudu I made for these, hoping to find a stick straight enough for a ramrod to force the empty cartridge out. As I reached them the kudu made for me with half a dozen plunges that sent me flying off for other cover. But Jock with feet planted against the tree hung on, and the kudu, turning furiously on him, stumbled, floundered, tripped, and came down with a crash amongst the crackling wood.

Once more like a flash Jock was over the fallen body and had fastened on the nose only to be shaken worse than before. The kudu literally flogged the ground with him, and for an instant I shut my eyes; it seemed as if the plucky dog would be beaten into pulp.

Then with a snort of fury the kudu, half-rising, gave its head a wild upward sweep, and flung Jock over its head and on to a low flat-topped thorn tree behind. The dog somersaulted slowly as he circled in the air, dropped on his back in the thorns some four metres from the ground, and came tumbling down through the branches. Surely the tree saved him, for it seemed as if such a throw must break his back. As it was he dropped with a sickening thump. Without a pause to breathe or even to look, he was in again, and trying once more for the nose.

The kudu lying partly on its side, with both hind legs hampered by the mass of dead wood, could not rise, but it swept the clear space in front with the terrible horns, and for some time kept Jock at bay. I tried stick after stick for a ramrod, but without success. At last, in desperation at seeing Jock once more hanging onto the kudu's nose, I hooked the lever on to a branch and setting my foot against the tree wrenched until the empty cartridge flew out.

In the last struggle, while I was busy with the rifle, the

106

kudu had moved, and it was then lying against one of the fallen trunks. The first swing to get rid of Jock had slogged him against the tree. The second swing swept him under it where a bend in the trunk raised it about 30 cm from the ground. There, with his feet planted firmly and his shoulder humped against the dead tree, Jock stood firm. The kudu with its head twisted back could put no weight to the pull; yet the wrenches it gave to free itself drew the nose and upper lip out like tough rubber and seemed to stretch Jock's neck visibly. I had to come round within a metre of them to avoid the risk of hitting Jock, and it seemed impossible for bone and muscle to stand the two or three terrible wrenches that I saw. The shot was the end. As the splendid head dropped slowly over, Jock let go his hold.

He had not uttered a sound except the grunts that were knocked out of him.

Jim Makokel'

Jim Makokel' was Jock's ally and champion. There was a great deal to like and something to admire in Jim. But, taking him all round, I am very much afraid that most people would consider him rather a bad lot. The fact of the matter is he belonged to another period and other conditions. He was a great passionate fighting man. Instead of wearing the cast-off clothing of the White man and peacefully driving bullock wagons along a transport road he should have been decked in his tribal finery of leopard skin and black ostrich feathers, and sharing in some wild war-dance, or, equipped with shield and assegais, be leading in some murderous fight.

Jim was out of date. He should have been one of the great Chaka's fighting guard — to rise as a leader of men, or be killed on the way. He had but one argument and one answer to everything: Fight! He was a survivor of a great fighting race and the turbulent blood that ran in his veins could not settle down into a placid stream merely because the Great White Queen had laid her hand upon his people and said, 'There shall be peace!' Chaka, the 'Black Napoleon' whose wars had cost South Africa over a million lives, had died — murdered by his brother Dingaan. Dingaan had been crushed by a gallant little band of Boers under Potgieter. Panda, the third of the three famous brothers had come and gone. Ketshwayo, the last of the great Zulu chiefs, after years of arrogant and unquestioned rule, loosed his straining impis at the people of the Great White Queen.

The awful day of Isandhlwana — where the 24th Regiment died almost to a man had bloodied the impis to madness. But Rorke's Drift and Kambula had followed those victories and told another tale. At Ulundi the tides met — the black and the white. And the kingdom and might of the house of Chaka were no more.

Jim had fought at Isandhlwana and could tell of an umfaan sent out to herd cattle within sight of the British camp in order to draw the troops out raiding while the impis crept round behind them. He could tell of the fight made by the redcoats as they were attacked hand to hand with stabbing assegais, ten and twenty to one, of one man in blue — a sailor — who was the last to die, fighting with his back to a wagon wheel against scores before him, and how he fell at last, stabbed in the back through the spokes of the wheel by one who had crept up behind.

Jim had fought at Rorke's Drift! He had gone on with the maddest of the victory-maddened lot to invade Natal and eat up the little garrison on the way. He could tell how seventy or eighty White men behind a little rampart of biscuit-tins and flour-bags had fought through the long and terrible hours, beating off five thousand of the Zulu best; how, from the

burning hospital, Sergeant Hook, V.C., and others carried sick and wounded through the flames into the laager; how a man in black with a long beard, Father Walsh, moved about with a calm face, speaking to some, helping others, carrying wounded back and cartridges forward — Father Walsh, who said, 'Don't swear, boys. Fire low'; how Lieutenants Chard and Bromhead — V.C.s too for that day's work — led and fought, and guided and heartened their heroic little band until the flour-bags and biscuit-tins stood lower than the pile of dead outside, and the Zulu host was beaten and Natal saved that day.

Jim had seen all. He knew the power of the Great White Queen and the way that her people fight. But peace was not for him or his kraal. Finally they were surrounded one night and massacred. Jim fought his way out, wounded and alone. Without kith or kin, cattle, king, or country, he fled to the Boer republic of Transvaal to live and work among White men for the first time in his life.

Wagon drivers often acquired a certain amount of reputation on the road or in the locality where they worked. But it was, as a rule, only a reputation as good or bad drivers. In Jim's case it was different. He was a character and had an individual reputation, which was exceptional. I had better say at once that not even his best friend would claim that that reputation was a good one. He was known as the best driver, the hardest fighter, and the worst drinker on the road.

His real name was Makokela, but in accordance with a common Zulu habit, it was usually abbreviated to Makokel'. Among a certain number of the White men — of the sort who never can get any name right — he was oddly enough known as McCorkindale. I called him Jim as a rule — Makokel' when relations were strained. The drivers found it safer to use his proper name. When anything had upset him it was not considered wise to take the liberty of shouting 'Jim'. The answer sometimes came in the shape of a hammering.

Many men had employed Jim before he came to me, and all had 'sacked' him for fighting, drinking, and the unbearable worry he caused. They told me this, and said that he gave more trouble than his work was worth. It may have been true. He certainly was a living test of patience, purpose, and

management, but I am glad that Jim never 'got the sack' from me. Why he did not, is not easy to say. Perhaps the circumstances under which he came to me and the hard knocks of an unkind fate pleaded for him. But it was not that alone. There was something in Jim himself — something good and fine, something that shone out from time to time, through his black skin and battered face, as the soul of a real man.

I met Jim during our first season in the bushveld. We were outspanned one night on the sand-hills overlooking Delagoa Bay among scores of other wagons dotted about in little camps — all loading or waiting for loads to transport to the Transvaal. Delagoa was not a good place to stay in those days. Liquor was cheap and bad, and there was very little in the way of law and order.

It was the third night of our stay, and the usual row was on. Shouts and cries, the beating of tom-toms, and shrill ear-piercing whistles, came from all sides. Near to us there was another camp of four wagons drawn up in close order, and as we sat talking and wondering at the strange

babel in the beautiful calm moonlight night, one sound was ever recurring, coming away out of all the rest with something in it that fixed our attention. It was the sound of two voices from the next camp.

One voice was a Zulu's — a great, deep, bull-throated voice. It was not raised but it carried far, with the ring and the lingering vibration of a big gong.

'Funa 'nyama, Inkos; funa 'nyama!' (I want meat, Chief; I want meat!) The request was repeated at intervals of a minute or two with deadly monotony and persistency.

The other, a White man's voice, grew more impatient, louder, and angrier with each refusal, but the Zulu paid no heed. A few minutes later the same request would be made, supplemented now and then with, 'I am hungry, Baas, I can't sleep. Meat! Meat! Meat!', or, 'Porridge and bread are for women and picaninnies. I am a man: I want meat, Baas, meat.' From the White man it was, 'Go to sleep, I tell you!', 'Be quiet, will you?', 'Shut up that row!', 'Be still, you drunken brute, or I'll tie you up!' and, 'You'll get twenty-five in a minute!'

It may have lasted half an hour when one of our party said, 'That's Bob's old driver, the big Zulu. There'll be a row tonight. He's with a foreigner chap from Natal now. New chums are always roughest on the drivers.'

In a flash I remembered Bob Saunderson's story of the driver who had caught the lion alive, and Bob's own words, 'a real fine worker, but a terror to drink, and always in trouble. He fairly wore me right out.'

A few minutes later there was a short scuffle, and the driver's voice could be heard protesting in the same deep low tone. They were tying him up to the wagon wheel for a flogging. Others were helping the White man, but the Black man was not resisting.

At the second thin whistling stroke someone said, 'That's a sjambok he's using, not a nek-strop!' A sjambok is a rawhide whip that would cut a bullock's hide. At about the eighth there was a wrench that made the wagon rattle, and the deep voice was raised in protest, 'Ow, Inkos!'

It made me choke. It was the first I knew of such things, and the horror of it was unbearable. But the man who had spoken before — a good man too, straight and strong, and trusted by Black and White — said, 'Sonny, you must not interfere between a man and his drivers here. It's hard sometimes, but we'd not live a day if they didn't know who was master.' I think we counted eighteen.

The White man looked about at the faces close to him — and stopped. He began slowly to untie the outstretched arms, and blustered out some threats. But no one said a word.

The noises died down as the night wore on, until the stillness was broken only by the desultory barking of a dog or the crowing of some awakened rooster who had mistaken the bright moonlight for the dawn. But for me there was one other sound for which I listened into the cool of morning with the quivering sensitiveness of a bruised nerve. Sometimes it was a long catchy sigh, and sometimes it broke into a groan just audible, like the faintest rumble of most distant surf. Twice in the long night there came the same request to one of the men near him, uttered in a deep clear unshaken voice and in a tone that was civil but firm, and strangely moving from its quiet indifference.

'Landela manzi, Umganaam!' (Bring water, friend!) was all he said; and each time the request was so quickly answered that I had the guilty feeling of being one in a great conspiracy

113

of silence. The hush was unreal; the stillness was alive with racing thoughts; the darkness was full of watching eyes.

There is, we believe, in the heart of every being a little germ of justice which men call conscience! If that be so, there must have been in the heart of the White man that night some uneasy movement — the first life-throb of the thought which one who had not yet written has since set down:

> Though I've belted you and flayed you,
> By the living God that made you,
> You're a better man than I am, Gunga Din!

The following afternoon I received an ultimatum. We had just returned from the town when from a group of drivers squatting round the fire there stood up one big fellow — a stranger — who raised his hand high above his head in Zulu fashion and gave their salute in the deep bell-like voice that there was no mistaking, 'Inkos! Bayete!'

He stepped forward, looking me all over, and announced with calm and settled conviction, 'I have come to work for you.' I said nothing. Then he rapped a chest like a big drum, and nodding his head with a sort of defiant confidence added in quaint English, 'My naam Makokela! Jim Makokel'! Yes! My catchum lion 'live! Makokela, me!'

He had heard that I wanted a driver, had waited for my return, and annexed me as his future 'baas' without a moment's doubt or hesitation.

I looked him over. Big, broad-shouldered, loose-limbed, and as straight as an assegai. A neck and head like a bull's; a face like a weather-beaten rock, storm-scarred and furrowed, rugged and ugly, but steadfast, massive and strong.

I nodded and said, 'You can come.'

Once more he raised his head aloft, and, simply and without a trace of surprise or gratification, said. 'Yes, you are my chief, I will work for you.' In his own mind it had been settled already. It had never been in doubt.

Jim — when sober — was a splendid worker and the most willing of servants, and, drunk or sober, he was always respectful in an independent, upstanding, hearty kind of way. His manner was as rough and rugged as his face and character.

114

Laughter came readily — laughter as strong and unrestrained as his bursts of passion.

To the other drivers he was what his nature and training had made him — not really a bully, but masterful and over-riding. He gave his orders with the curtness of a drill sergeant and the rude assurance of a savage chief. Walking, he walked his course, giving way for none of them. At the outspan or on the road or footpath he shouldered them aside as one walks through standing corn, not aggressively but with the superb indifference of right and habit unquestioned.

From time to time you do meet people like that. The world's their oyster, and the gift of a masterful and infinite confidence opens it every time. They walk through life taking of the best as a right, and the world unquestionably submits.

I had many troubles with Jim, but never on account of White men. Drunk or sober, there was never trouble there. It may have been Rorke's Drift and Ulundi that did it. But whatever it was, the question of Black and White was settled in his mind for ever. He was respectful, yet stood upright with the rough dignity of an unvanquished spirit. His troubles all came from drink, and the exasperation was at times so great, that on many occasions I heartily repented ever having taken him on. Warnings were useless, and punishments — well, the shiny new skin that made patterns in lines, stars and crosses on his back for the rest of his life, made answer for always upon that point.

The trouble began as soon as we reached a town, and he had a hundred excuses for going in, and a hundred more for not coming out. He had someone to see, boots to be mended, clothes to buy, or medicine to get.

The first precaution was to keep him at the wagons and put the towns and canteens 'out of bounds'. The last defence was to banish him entirely until he came back sober, and meanwhile set other men to do his work, paying them his wages in cash in his presence when he returned fit for duty.

'Is it as I told you? Is it just?' I would ask when this was done.

'It is just, Inkos.' There was never a trace of feeling to be detected when these affairs were squared off, but I knew how he hated the treatment, and it helped a little from time to time to keep him right.

The drink always produced a ravenous craving for meat, and when his money was gone and he had fought his fill and cleared out all opposition, he would come back to the wagons at any hour of the night, perhaps even two or three times between dark and dawn, to beg for meat. Warnings and orders had no effect whatever; he was unconscious of everything except the overmastering craving for meat. He would come to my wagon and begin that deadly monotonous recitation, 'Funa 'nyama, Inkos! Wanta meat, Baas!' There was a kind of hopeless determination in the tone conveying complete indifference to all consequences.

He was perfectly respectful. Every order to be quiet or go away or go to bed was received with the most respectful of salutations, but in the very next breath would come the old monotonous request, 'Funa 'nyama Inkos', just as if he was saying it for the first time. The persistency was maddening and there was no remedy, for it was not the result of voluntary or even conscious effort on his part. It was a result of his physical condition.

When the meat was there I gave it, and he would sit by the fire for hours eating incredible quantities. But it was not always possible to satsify him in that way, and then the night became one long torment. The spell of rest might extend from a quarter of an hour to an hour. From the dead sleep of downright weariness I would be roused by the deep, far-reaching voice, 'Funa 'nyama, Inkos', and waking I would find Jim standing beside me remorselessly urging the same request in Zulu, in broken English, and in Dutch — 'My wanta meat, Baas', 'Will fleisch krij, Baas', and the old, old, hatefully familiar explanation of the difference between 'man's food' and 'picanins' food', interspersed with grandiose declarations that he was 'Makokela — Jim Makokel' ', who 'catchum lion 'live'. Sometimes he would expand this into comparisons between himself and the other men, much to their disadvantage. On these occasions he invariably worked round to his private grievances, and expressed his candid opinions of Sam.

Sam was the driver whom I usually set to do Jim's neglected work. He was a 'mission boy', Christian, very proper in his behaviour, but a weakling and not much good at work. Jim would enumerate all Sam's shortcomings: how he got his oxen mixed up on dark nights and could not pick them out of the herd; how he stuck in the drifts and had to be 'double-spanned' and pulled out by Jim; how he once lost his way in the bush; and how he upset the wagon coming down the Devil's Shoot.

Jim had once brought down the Berg from Spitzkop a loaded wagon on which there was a cottage piano packed standing upright. The road was an awful one, and few drivers could have handled so top-heavy a load without capsizing. To Jim the feat was one without parallel in the history of wagon driving, and when drunk he usually coupled it with his other great achievement of catching a lion alive. His contempt for Sam's misadventure on the Devil's Shoot was therefore great, and to it was added resentment against Sam's respectability and superior education, which the latter was able to rub in by ostentatiously reading his Bible aloud.

117

When his detailed indictment of Sam was complete Jim would wind up with 'My catchum lion 'live. My bling pan-yanna fon Diskop (bring piano from Spitzkop). My naam Makokela: Jim Makokel'. Sam no good; Sam leada Bible (Sam reads the Bible). Sam no good!' The intensity of conviction and the gloomy disgust put into the last reference to Sam are not to be expressed in words.

The Allies

To Jim there were three big divisions of the human race —
White men, Zulus and the rest. Zulu, old or young, was
greeted by him as equal, friend and comrade. White men
he respected, but the rest were trash. He cherished a most
particular contempt for the Shangaans and Chopis, and the
sight of them stirred him to contempt and pricked him to
hostilities. It was not long before Jim discovered that Jock
needed only a little encouragement to share his views.

It was very important to me that Jock should treat strange
Black men with suspicion and keep them off the premises. I
was glad that he did it by his own choice and instinct; but at
the same time I did feel he should be taught where to draw
the line. Jim made the already difficult task practically
impossible by egging Jock on.

As far as I know the first incident arose out of the intrusion
of a strange Black man at one of the outspans. Jock objected,
and he forced the man back step by step — doing the same
feinting rushes that he practised with game — until the
terrified man tripped over a camp stool and sat plump down
on the three-legged pot of porridge. I did not see it, for Jock
was, as usual, quite silent. It was a roar from Jim that roused
me. Jock was standing with his head on one side and his face
full of interest, as if he would dearly love another romp in;
and the drivers were reeling and rolling about on the grass,
helpless with laughter.

A dog is just as quick as a child to find out when he can

take liberties. He knows that laughter and serious disapproval do not go together; and Jock with the backing of the drivers thoroughly enjoyed himself. That was how it began, and by degrees it developed into what became known as the Shangaan gang trick.

One day a gang of about thirty Shangaan miners each carrying his load of blankets, clothing, pots, billies and other valuables on his head, was coming in single file along a footpath some twenty metres away from the wagons. Jock strolled out and sat himself down in the middle of the path. The leader of the gang was suspicious and shied off wide into the veld. He passed in a semicircle round Jock, a good ten metres away, and came safely back to the path again. The dog with his nose in the air merely eyed him with a look of humorous interest and mild curiosity. The second miner made the loop shorter, and the third made it shorter still, as they found their alarm and suspicions unjustified.

As each came along, the size of the loop was lessened until they passed in safety almost brushing against Jock's nose. And still he never budged. But as each man approached, he looked up at his face and, slowly turning his head, followed him round with his eyes until he re-entered the path.

There was something extremely funny in the mechanical regularity with which his head swung round. It was so funny that not only did the drivers at the wagons notice it and laugh but the unsuspecting Shangaans themselves shared the joke.

The long heavy bundles on their heads made turning round a slow process, so that, except for the first half-dozen, they were content to enjoy what they saw in front and to know by the laughter from behind that the joke had been repeated all down the line.

The last one walked calmly by, but as he did so there came one short muffled bark from Jock, and he sprang out and nipped the unsuspecting Shangaan from behind. The man let out a yell that made the whole gang jump and clutch wildly at their toppling bundles, and Jock raced along the footpath, leaping, gurgling and snapping behind each one, scattering them this way and that, in a romp of wild enjoyment.

The shouts of the scared men, the clatter of the tins as their bundles toppled down, the scrambling and scratching as they clawed the ground pretending to pick up stones or sticks to stop his rushes, and the ridiculous rout of the thirty Shangaans in every direction, were too much for my principles and far too much for my gravity. To be quite honest, I weakened badly, and from that day on preferred to look another way when Jock sallied out to inspect a gang of Shangaans. Between them Jim and Jock had beaten me.

But the weakening brought its own punishment and the joke was not far from causing a tragedy.

Many times while lying some way off in the shade of a tree or under another wagon I heard Jim, all unconscious of my presence, call in a low deep voice, almost a whisper, 'Jock; Jock: Shangaans!' Jock's head was up in a moment, and a romp of some sort followed unless I intervened. After-wards, when Jock was deaf, Jim used to reach out and pull his foot or throw a handful of sand or a bunch of grass to rouse him, and when Jock's head switched up Jim's big black fist pointing to their common enemy was quite enough.

Jim had his faults, but getting others into mischief while keeping out of it himself was not one of them. If he egged Jock on, he was more than ready to stand by him.

121

There was a day outside Barberton which I remember well. Jim was lying under his wagon with his chin resting on his arms, staring steadily at the glistening corrugated iron roofs of the town, as morose and unapproachable as a surly old watch-dog. From the tent of my wagon I saw him raise his head, and following his glance, picked out a row of bundles against the skyline. Presently a long string of about fifty time-expired miners came into sight. Jim, on his hands and knees, scrambled over to where Jock lay asleep, and shook him; for this incident occurred after Jock had become deaf.

'Shangaans, Jock; Shangaans! Kill them; kill, kill, kill!' said Jim in gusty ferocious whispers. It must have seemed as if Fate had kindly provided an outlet for the rebellious rage and the craving for a fight that were consuming him.

I had had a lot of trouble with Jim that day, and this annoyed me, but my angry call to stop was unavailing. Jim, pretending not to understand, made no attempt to stop Jock, but contented himself with calling to him to come back, and Jock, stone deaf, trotted evenly along with his head, neck, back, and tail, all level — an old trick of Jess's which generally meant trouble for some one.

Slowing down as he neared the Shangaans he walked quietly on until he headed off the leader, and there he stood across the path. It was just the same as before. The men, finding that he did nothing, merely stepped aside to avoid bumping against him. They were taking their purchases to their kraals. Gaudy blankets, collections of bright tin billies and mugs, tin plates, three-legged pots, clothing, hats, and even small tin trunks painted brilliant yellow, helped to make up their huge bundles.

The last man was wearing a pair of Royal Artillery trousers, and I have no doubt he regarded it ever afterwards as nothing less than a calamity that they were not safely stowed away in his bundle. It was from the seat of these too ample bags that Jock took a good mouthful; and it was the miner's frantic jump, rather than Jock's tug, that made the piece come out. The sudden fright and the attempts to face about quickly caused several downfalls. The clatter of these spread the panic; and on top of it all came Jock's charge along the broken line, and the excited shouts of those who thought they were going to be worried to death.

But there came a very unexpected change.

One big Shangaan had drawn from his bundle a brand new side-axe. I saw the bright steel head flash as he held it menacingly aloft by the short handle and marched towards Jock. There was a scrambling sound from under the wagon and Jim rushed out. In his right hand he brandished a tough stout fighting stick. In his left I was horrified to see an assegai, and well I knew that, with the fighting fury on him, he would think nothing of using it.

The Shangaan saw him coming, and stopped. Still facing Jim, and with the axe raised and feinting repeatedly to throw it, he began to back away. Jim never paused for a second. He came straight on with wild leaps and blood-curdling yells in Zulu fighting fashion and ended with a bound that seemed to drop him right on top of the other. The stick came down with a whirr and a crash that crimped every nerve in my body; and the Shangaan dropped like a log.

I had shouted myself hoarse at Jim, but he heard or heeded nothing. He wrenched the axe from the kicking man and, without pause, went headlong for the next Shangaan he saw. Everything went wrong: the more I shouted and the

123

harder I ran, the worse the row. The Shangaans seemed to think I had joined in and was directing operations against them. Jim seemed to be inspired to wilder madness by my shouts and gesticulations; and Jock — well, Jock, at any rate had not the remotest doubt as to what he should do. When he saw me and Jim in full chase behind him, his plain duty was to go in for all he was worth; and he did it.

It was half an hour before I got Jim back. He was as unmanageable as a runaway horse. He had walloped the majority of the fifty himself. He had broken his own two sticks and used up a number of theirs. On his forehead there was a small cut and a lump like half an orange; and on the back of his head another cut left by the sticks of the enemy when eight or ten had rallied once in a half-hearted attempt to stand against him.

It was strange how Jim, even in that mood, yielded to the touch of one whom he regarded as his 'Inkos'. I could not have forced him back.

He yielded to the light grip of my hand on his wrist and walked freely along with me. But a fiery bounding vitality possessed him, and all the time there came from him a torrent of excited gabble in pure Zulu, punctuated and paragraphed by bursting allusions to 'dogs of Shangaans', 'axes', 'sticks', and 'Jock'.

Near the wagons we passed over the 'battlefield', and a huge guffaw of laughter broke from Jim as we came on the abandoned impedimenta of the defeated enemy. Jim looked on it all as the spoils of war, and wanted to stop and gather in his loot there and then. When I pressed on, he shouted to the other drivers to come out and collect the booty.

But my chief anxiety was to end the wretched escapade as quickly as possible and get the Shangaans on their way again. So I sent Jim back to his place under the wagon, and told the cook to give him the rest of my coffee and half a cup of sugar to provide him with something else to think of and to calm him down.

After a wait of half an hour or so, a head appeared just over the rise, and then another, and another, at irregular intervals and at various points. They were scouting very cautiously before venturing back again. I sat in the tent wagon out of sight and kept quiet, hoping that in a few minutes they would gain confidence, collect their goods, and go their way again. Jim, lying flat under the wagon, was much lower than I was, and — continuing his gabble to the others — saw nothing. Unfortunately he looked round just as a scared face peered cautiously over the top of an antheap. The temptation was, I suppose, irresistible. He scrambled to his knees with a pretence of starting afresh, let out one ferocious yell that made my hair stand up, and in that second every head bobbed down and the field was deserted once more.

If this went on there could be but one ending: the police would be appealed to, Jim arrested, and I should spend days hanging about the courts waiting for a trial from which the noble Jim would probably emerge with three months' hard labour. So I sallied out as my own herald of peace. But the position was more difficult than it looked: As soon as the Shangaans saw my head appearing over the rise, they scattered like chaff before the wind, and ran as if they would never stop. They evidently took me for the advance guard in a fresh attack. I stood upon an antheap and waved and called, but each shout resulted in a fresh spurt and each movement only made them more suspicious. It seemed a hopeless case, and I gave it up.

125

On the way back to the wagons, however, I thought of Sam — Sam, with his neatly patched European clothes, his slack lanky figure and serious timid face. Sam would surely be the right envoy; even the routed Shangaans would feel that there was nothing to fear there. But Sam was by no means anxious to earn laurels, and it was a poor-looking weak-kneed and much dejected scarecrow that dragged its way reluctantly out into the veld to hold parley with the routed enemy that day.

At the first mention of Sam's name Jim had twitched round with a snort, but the humour of the situation tickled him when he saw the too obvious reluctance with which his rival received the honour conferred on him. To Sam's relief, the Shangaans seemed to view him merely as a decoy, even more dangerous than I was. They were widely scattered more than a kilometre away when Sam came in sight. A brief pause followed in which they looked anxiously around, and then, after some aimless dashes about like a startled troop of buck, they seemed to find the line of flight and headed off in a long string down the valley towards the river.

Now, no one had ever run away from Sam before, and the exhilarating sight so encouraged him that he marched boldly on after them. Goodness knows when, if ever, they would have stopped, if Sam had not met a couple of other Black men whom the Shangaans had passed and induced them to turn back and reassure the fugitives.

An hour later Sam came back in mild triumph, at the head of the Shangaan gang, and stood guard and superintended while they collected their scattered goods — all except the axe that caused the trouble. That they failed to find. The owner may have thought it wise to make no claim on me. Sam, if he remembered it, would have seen the Shangaans and all their belongings burned in a pile rather than raise so delicate a question with Jim. I had forgotten all about it — being anxious only to end the trouble and get the Shangaans off; and that villain Jim 'lay low'. At the first outspan from Barberton next day I saw him carving his mark on the handle, unabashed, under my very nose.

The next time Jim got drunk he added something to his opinion of Sam:

'Sam no good: Sam leada Bible! Shangaan, Sam; Shangaan!'

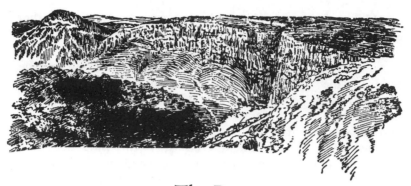

The Berg

The last day of each trip in the bushveld was always a day of trial and hard work for man and beast. The Drakensberg stood up before us like an impassable barrier.

On a flat-topped terrace-like spur where the last outspan was, we took breath, halved our loads, double-spanned, and pulled ourselves together for the last big climb.

To those who do not know, there is not much difference between spans of oxen; and the driving of them seems merely a matter of brute strength in arm and lung. One span looks like another. The weird unearthly yells of the drivers, the cracks — like rifle-shots — of the long lashes, and the hum and thud of the more cruel doubled whip, seem to be all that is needed. But it is not so. Heart and training in the cattle, skill and judgement in the driver, are needed too; for the Berg is a searching test of man and beast.

It was on the Drakensberg that I first saw what a really first-class man can do. There were many wagons facing the pass that day. Portions of loads, dumped off to ease the pull, dotted the roadside; tangles of disordered maddened spans blocked the way; and fragments of yokes, skeys, strops, and reims, and broken disselbooms, told the tale of trouble.

Old Charlie Roberts came along with his two wagons. He was 'old' to us — being nearly fifty. He was also stout and in poor health. We buried him at Pilgrim's Rest a week later.

Charlie walked slowly up past us, to 'take a squint at things', as he put it, and see if it was possible to get past the stuck wagons. A little later he started, making three loads of his two and going up with single spans of eighteen oxen each, because the other wagons, stuck in various places on the road, did not give him room to work double spans.

To us it seemed madness to attempt with eighteen oxen a harder task than we and others were essaying with thirty. We would have waited until the road ahead was clear.

We were half-way up when we saw old Charlie coming along steadily and without any fuss at all. He had no second driver to help him and he did no shouting. He walked along

heavily and with difficulty beside the span, playing the long whip lightly about as he gave the word to go or called quietly to individual oxen by name, but he did not touch them. When he paused to 'blow' them he leaned heavily on his whip-stick to rest himself. We were stopped by some break in the gear and were completely blocking the road when he caught up.

Anyone else would have waited. He pulled out into the rough sideling track on the slope below, to pass us. Even a good span with a good driver may well come to grief in trying to pass another that is stuck — for the sight and example are demoralising — but old Charlie did not turn a hair. He went steadily on, giving a brisker call and touching up his oxen here and there with light flicks.

The track he took was merely the scorings made by skidding wagons coming down the mountain. It was so steep and rough there that a pull of ten metres between the spells for breath was all one could hope for; and many were thankful to have done much less. At the second pause, as they were passing us, one of his oxen turned, leaning inwards against the chain, and looked back. Old Charlie remarked quietly, 'I thought he would chuck it; only bought him last week. He's got no heart.'

He walked along the span up to the shirking animal, which continued to glare back at him in a frightened way, and touched it behind with the butt of his long whip-stick to bring it up to the yoke. The ox started forward into place with a jerk, but eased back again slightly as Charlie went back to his place. At the next stop it lay back worse than before.

Not one driver in a hundred would have done then what he did. They would have tried other courses first. Charlie dropped his whip quietly and outspanned the ox and its mate, saying to me as I gave him a hand, 'When I strike a rotter, I chuck him out before he spoils the others.' In another ten minutes he and his stalwarts had left us behind.

Old Charlie knew his oxen — each one of them, their characters, and what they could do. I think he loved them too. At any rate, it was his care for them that day — handling them himself instead of leaving it to his drivers that brought

out the fever that killed him. It was his last trek.

The driving of bullocks is not an exalted occupation. It is a very humble calling indeed. Yet, if one is able to learn, there are things worth learning in that useful school. The men never trouble themselves with introspections and analyses, and if you asked one of them the secret of success, he might tell you 'Common sense and hard work'.

Among themselves, when the prime topics of loads, rates, grass, water and disease have been disposed of, there is as much interest in talking about their own and each other's oxen as there is in babies at a mothers meeting. Spans are compared; individual oxen discussed in minute detail; and the reputations of 'front oxen', in pairs or singly, are canvassed.

No two oxen are alike. You find them nervous and lethargic, timid and bold, independent and sociable, exceptional and ordinary, willing and sulky, restless and content, staunch and faint-hearted — just like human beings. I can remember some of them now far better than many of the men known then and since. I remember Achmoed and Bakir, the big after-oxen who carried the disselboom contentedly through the trek and were spared all other work to save them for emergencies. At a word they heaved together — their great backs bent like bows and their giant strength thrown in to hoist the wagon from the deepest hole and up the steepest hill. They were the

stand-by in the worst descents, lying back on their haunches to hold the wagon up when brakes could do no more. Inseparable always — even when outspanned the two old comrades walked together.

There was little Zole, contented, sociable and short of wind. There was Bantom, the big red ox with the white band, lazy and selfish, with an enduring evil obstinacy that was simply incredible. There was Rooiland, the light red, with yellow eyeballs and topped horns, a fierce, wild, unapproachable, unappeasable creature, restless and impatient, always straining to start, always moaning fretfully when delayed. And then there was old Zwaartland, the coal-black front ox, and the best of all. The sober, steadfast leader of the span, who knew his work by heart and answered with quickened pace to any call of his name. He stood out from all the rest. The massive horns, like one huge spiral pin passed through his head, 2,5 metres from tip to tip; the clean limbs and small neat feet moving with the quick precision of a buck's tread; and the large grey eyes so soft and clear and deep.

There was a day at Kruger's Post when everything seemed small beside the figure of one black front ox, who held his ground when all others failed. The wagon had sunk to the bed-plank in gluey turf, and, although the whole load had been taken off, three spans linked together failed to move it. For eight hours that day we tried to dig and pull it out, but forty-four oxen on that soft greasy flat toiled in vain. The long string of bullocks, desperate from failure and bewilderment, swayed in the middle from side to side to seek escape from the flying whips. The unyielding wagon held them at one end, and the front oxen strove to hold them true at the other. Seven times that day we changed, trying to find a mate who would stand with Zwaartland, but he wore them all down. He broke their hearts and stood it out alone. I looked at the ground afterwards. It was grooved in long parallel lines where the swaying spans had pulled him backwards, with his four feet clawing the ground in the effort to hold them true. But he had never once turned or wavered.

And there was a day at Sand River, when we saw a different picture. The wagons were empty, yet as we came up out of the stony drift, Bantom the sulky hung lazily back, dragging on his yoke and throwing the span out of line. Jim curled the big whip round him, without any good effect, and when the span stopped for a breather in the deep narrow road, he lay down and refused to budge. There was no reason in the world for it except the animal's obstinate sulky temper. When the whip — the giraffe-hide thong, doubled into a heavy loop — produced no effect, the driver took the yoke off to see if freedom would tempt the animal to rise. It did. At the first touch of the whip Bantom jumped up and charged them. Seeing that there was nothing at all the matter, the driver inspanned him and made a fresh start – not touching him again for fear of another fit of sulks; but at the first call on the team, down he went again.

Many are the stories of cruelty to oxen, and I had never understood how human beings could be so fiendishly cruel as to do some of the things that one heard of. But what I saw

that day threw some light on these questions.

There were two considerations which governed the whole case. The first was that as long as the ox lay there it was impossible to move the wagon, and there was no way for the others to pass it. The second was that the ox was free, strong and perfectly well, and all he had to do was to get up and walk.

The drivers from the other wagons came up to lend a hand and clear the way so that they might get on. Sometimes three were at it together with their double whips; and, before they could be stopped, sticks and stones were used to hammer the animal on the head and horns, along the spine, on the hocks and shins, and wherever he was supposed to have feeling. Then he was tied by the horns to the trek-chain, so that the span would drag him bodily; but not once did he make the smallest effort to rise. The road was merely a gutter scoured out by the floods and it was not possible either to drag the animal up the steep sides or to leave him and go on — the wagon would have had to pass over him. And all this time he was outspanned and free to go; but would not stir.

Then they doubled the tail and bit it; very few bullocks will stand that, but Bantom never winced. They took their clasp knives and used them as spurs — not stabbing to do real injury, but pricking enough to draw blood in the fleshy parts, where it would be most felt. He twitched to the pricks — but nothing more. They made a fire close behind him, and as the wood blazed up, the heat seemed unendurable; the smell of singed hair was strong, and the flames, centimetres away, seemed to roast the flesh. One of the drivers took a brand and pressed the glowing red coal against the inside of the hams; but, beyond a vicious kick at the fire, there was no result. Then they tried to suffocate him, gripping the mouth and nostrils so that he could not breathe. But, when the limit of endurance was reached and even the spectators tightened up with a sense of suffocation, a savage shake of the head always freed it — the brute was too strong for them.

For the better part of an hour the struggle went on, but there was not the least sign of yielding on Bantom's part, and the string of waiting wagons grew longer, and many others gathered round watching, helping or suggest-

134

ing. At last someone brought a bucket of water, and into this Bantom's muzzle was thrust as far as it would go, and reims passed through the ears of the bucket were slipped round his horns so that he could not shake himself free at will. We stood back and watched the animal's sides for signs of breathing. For an incredible time he held out. But at last with a sudden plunge he was up. A bubbling

muffled bellow came from the bucket; the drivers let go the reims, and the terrified animal, ridding himself of the bucket after a frantic struggle, stood with legs apart and eyeballs starting from the sockets, shaking like a reed.

But nothing that had happened revealed the vicious ingrained obstinacy of the animal's nature so clearly as the last act in the struggle. It stood passive, and apparently beaten, while the drivers inspanned it again. But at the first call to the team to start, and without a touch to provoke its temper again, it dropped down once more. Not one of all those looking on would have believed it possible; but there it was! In the most deliberate manner the challenge was again flung down, and the whole fight begun afresh.

We felt really desperate. One could think of nothing but to repeat the bucket trick; for it was the only one that had succeeded at all. The bucket had been flung aside on the stones as the ox freed itself, and one of the drivers picked it up to fetch more water. But no more was needed.

135

The rattle of the bucket brought Bantom to his feet with a terrified jump, and flinging his whole weight into the yoke, he gave the wagon a heave that started the whole span, and they went out at a run.

It would have taken a good man to handle Bantom, at any time — even in the beginning. But, full-grown, and confirmed in his evil ways, only the butcher could make anything out of him.

And only the butcher did!

Paradise Camp

There is a spot on the edge of the Drakensberg which we made our summer quarters. When September came round and the sun swung higher in the steely blue sky and the little creeks were running dry and the water-holes became saucers of cracked mud; when the whole country smelt of fine impalpable dust; it was a relief to quit the bushveld, and even the hunting was given up almost without regret.

Paradise Camp perched on the very edge of the mountain range. Behind us rolled green slopes to the feet of the higher peaks, and in front of us lay the bushveld. The breeze blew cool and fresh there. The waters trickled and splashed in every little break or tumbled with steady roar down the greater gorges. Deep pools, fringed with masses of ferns, smooth as mirrors or flecked with dancing sunlight, were set like brilliants in the silver chain of each little stream; and rocks and pebbles, wonderful in their colours, were magnified and glorified into polished gems by the sparkling water.

But Nature has her moods, and it was not always thus at Paradise Camp. When the cold mist-rains, like wet grey fogs, swept over us and for a week blotted out creation, it was neither pleasant nor safe to grope along the edge of the Berg, in search of strayed cattle — wet and cold, unable to see, and checked from time to time by a keener straighter gust that leapt up over the unseen precipice a few metres off.

And there was still another mood when the summer

137

rains set in and the storms burst over us, and the lightning stabbed viciously in all directions. The crackling crash of the thunder made it seem as if the very Berg itself must be split and shattered. Then the rivers rose; the roar of waters was all around us; and Paradise Camp was isolated from the rest by floods which no man would lightly face.

Paradise Camp stood on the edge of the kloof where the nearest timber grew. Tumbling Waters, where stood the thousand grey sandstone sentinels of strange fantastic shapes, was three kilometres away facing Black Bluff, the highest point of all, and The Camel, The Wolf, The Sitting Hen, and scores more, rough casts in rock by Nature's hand, stood there. Close below us was the Bathing Pool, with its six metres of purest water, its three rock-ledge 'springboards', and its banks of moss and canopies of tree ferns.

Further down, the stream spread in a thousand pools and rapids over a kilometre of black bedrock and then poured in one broad sheet over Graskop Falls. And still further down were the Mac Mac Falls, a hundred metres straight down into the rock-strewn gorge, where the walls were draped with staghorn moss, like countless folds of delicate green lace, bespangled by the spray. We were felling and slipping timber for the gold-fields then, and it was in these surroundings that the work was done.

It was a Sunday morning, and I was lying on my back on a sack-stretcher taking it easy, when Jock gave a growl and trotted out. Presently I heard voices in the next hut and wondered who the visitors were. Then a cold nose was poked against my cheek and I looked round to see Jess's little eyes and flickering ears within centimetres of my face. For the moment she did not look cross, but as if a faint smile of welcome were flitting across a soured face. Then she trotted back to the other hut where Ted was patting Jock and trying to trace a likeness to the Rat.

It was a long time since mother and son had been together, and if the difference between them was remarkable, the likeness seemed to me more striking still. Jock had grown up by himself and made himself. He was so different from other dogs that I had forgotten how much he owed to good old Jess. But now that they were once more side

138

by side everything he did and had done recalled the likeness and yet showed the difference between them. Many times as we moved about the camp or worked in the woods they walked or stood together, sometimes sniffing along some spoor and sometimes waiting and watching for us to come up — handsome son and ugly mother. Ugly she might be, with her little fretful hostile eyes, her uncertain ever-moving ears, and her silent, sour cross nature. But stubborn fidelity and reckless courage were hers too; and all the good Jock had in him came from Jess.

To see them side by side was enough. Every line in his golden brindled coat had its counterpart in her dull markings. His jaw was hers, with a difference. Every whit as determined but without the savage look. His eyes were hers — brown to black as the moods changed — yet not fretful and cross, but serenely observant, when quiet, and black, hot and angry, when roused. His ears were hers — and yet different; not shifting, flickering and ever on the move, nor flattened back with the look of most uncertain temper, but sure in their movements and faithful reflectors of more sober moods and a more balanced temper.

The work kept us close to camp and we gave no thought to shooting; yet Jess and Jock had some good sport together.

Once they caught an ant-bear in the open, and there was a rough-and-tumble. We had no weapons — not even sticks — with us, and the dogs had it all to themselves.

Once they killed a tiger-cat. We heard the rush and the row, and when we came up to them it was all over and they were

139

tugging and tearing at the lifeless black and white body. Jess at the throat and Jock at the stomach. They thoroughly enjoyed it and searched the place afresh every time we passed it, as regularly as a boy looks about where he once picked up a sixpence.

One day while at work in the woods there came to us a grizzled worn-looking old Black man, whose head ring of polished black wax attested his dignity as a kehla. He carried an old musket and was attended by two youngsters armed with throwing-sticks and a hunting assegai each. He appeared to be a 'somebody' in a small way, and we knew at a glance that he had not come for nothing.

There is a certain courtesy and a good deal of formality observed among the Black men of Africa which is appreciated by very few of the White men who come in contact with them. One reason for this failure in appreciation is that this type of courtesy is in its method and expression sometimes just the reverse of what we consider proper. The old man, passing and ignoring the group of drivers, came towards us as we sat in the shade for the midday rest, and slowly came to a stand a few metres off, leaning on his long flint-lock quietly taking stock of us each in turn, and

waiting for us to inspect him. Then, after three or four minutes of this, he proceeded to salute us separately with 'Sakubona, Umlungu!' delivered with measured deliberation at intervals of about a quarter of a minute. Each salutation was accompanied by the customary upward movement of the head — their respectful equivalent of our nod or bow. When he had done the round, his two attendants took their turns, and when this was over, and another long pause had served to mark his respect, he drew back a few paces, and, tucking his loin skins comfortably under him, squatted down. Ten minutes more elapsed before he allowed his eyes to wander absently round towards the drivers and finally to settle on them for a repetition of the performance that we had been favoured with. But in this case it was they who led off with the 'Sakubona, Umganaam!' which he acknowledged with the raising of the head and a soft murmur of contented recognition, 'A-hé'.

Once more there was silence for a spell, while he waited to be questioned in the customary manner, and to give an account of himself, before it would be courteous or proper to introduce the subject of his visit. It was Jim's voice that broke the silence — clear and imperative, as usual, but not uncivil. It always was Jim who cut in, as those do who are naturally impatient of delays and formalities.

'Velapi, Umganaam?' (Where do you come from, friend?) he asked, putting the question which is recognised as courteously providing the stranger with an opening to give an account of himself. He is expected and required to do so to their satisfaction before he in turn can ask all about them, their occupations, homes, destination and master, and his occupation, purpose and possessions.

The talk went round in low exchanges until at last the old man moved closer and joined the circle. The other voices dropped out, only to be heard once in a while in some brief question or that briefest of all comments, 'Ow!' It may mean anything, according to the tone, but it was clearly sympathetic on that occasion. The old man's voice went on monotonously in a low-pitched impassive tone; but the drivers hung intent on every word to the end. Then one or two questions, briefly answered in the same tone of

141

detached philosophic indifference, brought their talk to a close. The old fellow tapped his carved wood snuff-box with the carefully preserved long yellowish nail of one forefinger, and pouring some snuff into the palm of his hand, drew it into each nostril in turn with long luxurious sniffs; and then, resting his arms on his knees, he relapsed into complete silence.

We called the drivers to start work again, and they came away, as is their custom, without a word or look towards the man whose story had held them for the last half-hour. Nor did he speak or stir, but sat on unmoved, a picture of stoical indifference. But who can say if it be indifference or fatalism or the most astute diplomacy?

We asked no questions, for we knew it was no accident that had brought the old man our way. He wanted something, and we would learn soon enough what it was. So we waited.

As we gathered round the fallen tree to finish the cleaning and slip it down to the track Jim remarked irrelevantly that leopards were 'skelms', and it was his conviction that there were a great many in the kloofs round about. At intervals during the next hour or so he dropped other scraps about leopards and their ways, and how to get at them and what good sport it was, winding up with a short account of how two seasons back an English 'capitaine' had been killed by one only a few kilometres away.

Jim was no diplomat. He had leopard on the brain, and showed it. So, when I asked him bluntly what the old man had been talking about, the whole story came out. There was a leopard — it was of course the biggest ever seen — which had been preying on the old chief's kraal for the last six months. Dogs, goats and sheep innumerable had disappeared, even fowls were not despised. Only two days ago the climax had been reached when, in the cool of the afternoon and in defiance of the yelling herdboy, it had slipped into the herd at the drinking place and carried off a calf — a heifer-calf too. The old man was poor. The leopard had nearly ruined him, and he had come up to see if we, 'who were great hunters', would come down and kill the thief, or at least lend him a leopard trap, as he could not afford to buy one.

142

In the evening when we returned to camp we found the old fellow there, and heard the story told with the same patient resignation or stoical indifference with which he had told it to the drivers.

The chance seemed good enough, and we decided to go. Leopards were plentiful enough and were often to be heard at night in the kloofs below, but they are extremely wary animals and in the inhabited parts rarely move about by day. However, the marauding habits and the audacity of this fellow were full of promise.

The following afternoon we set off with our guns and blankets, a little food for two days, and the leopard trap. By nightfall we had reached the foot of the Berg by paths and ways which you might think only a baboon could follow.

It was moonlight, and we moved along through the heavily timbered kloofs in single file behind the shadowy figure of the shrivelled old chief. His years seemed no handicap to him, as with long easy soft-footed strides he went on hour after hour.

The air was delightfully cool and sweet with the fresh smells of the woods. The damp carpet of moss and dead leaves dulled the sound of our more blundering steps. Now and again through the thick canopy of evergreens we caught glimpses of the moon, and in odd places the light threw stumps or rocks into quaint relief or turned some tall bare trunk into a ghostly sentinel of the forest.

We had crossed the last of the many mountain streams and reached open ground when the old chief stopped, and pointing to the face of a high krans, said that somewhere up there was a cave which was the leopard's home, and it was from this safe refuge that he raided the countryside.

143

We started on again down an easy slope passing through some bush, and at the bottom came on level ground thinly covered with big shady trees and scattered undergrowth. As we walked briskly through the flecked and dappled light and shade, we were startled by the sudden and furious rush of Jess and Jock off the path and away into the scrub on the left; and immediately after there was a grunting noise, a crashing and scrambling, and then one sharp clear yelp of pain from one of the dogs. There were other sounds in the bush — something like a faint scratching, and something like smothered sobbing grunts, but so indistinct as to be more ominous and disquieting than absolute silence.

'He has killed the dogs', the old chief said, in a low voice.

But as he said it there was a rustle in front, and something came out towards us. The guns were up and levelled instantly, but dropped again when we saw it was a dog. Jess came back limping badly and stopping every few paces to shake her head and rub her mouth against her fore-paws. She was in great pain and breathed out faint barely audible whines from time to time.

We waited for minutes, but Jock did not appear. As the curious sounds still came from the bush we moved forward in open order, very slowly and with infinite caution. As we got closer, scouting each bush and open space, the sounds grew clearer, and suddenly it came to me that it was the noise of a body being dragged and the grunting breathing of a dog. I called sharply to Jock and the sound stopped. Taking a few paces forward, I saw him in a moon-lit space turning round and round on the pivot of his hind legs and swinging or dragging something much bigger than himself.

Jim gave a yell and shot past me, plunging his assegai into the object and shouting, 'Porcupine, porcupine', at the top of his voice. We were all round it in a couple of seconds, but I think the porcupine was as good as dead even before Jim had stabbed it.

This encounter with the porcupine gave us a better chance of getting the leopard than we ever expected — too good a chance to be neglected. So, we cut the animal up and used the worthless parts to bait the big trap, having first dragged them across the veld for a good distance each way to leave a blood spoor which would lead the leopard up to the trap. This, with the quantity of blood spread about in the fight, lying right in the track of his usual prowling ought to attract his attention, we thought; and we fastened the trap to a big tree, making an avenue of bushes up to the bait so that he would have to walk right over the trap hidden under the dead leaves, in order to get at the bait. We hoped that, if it failed to hold, it would at least wound him badly enough to enable us to follow him up in the morning.

Jock was none the worse for his fight with the porcupine and was the picture of contentment as he lay beside me in the ring facing the fire. But Jess was a puzzle. From the time that she had come hobbling back to us, carrying her one foot in the air and stopping to rub her mouth on her paws, we had been trying to find out what was the matter. The foot trouble was clear enough, for there was a quill 35 centimetres long still piercing the ball of her foot. Fortunately it had not been driven far through and the hole was small, so that once it was drawn and the foot bandaged she got along fairly well. It was not the foot that was troubling her. All through the evening she kept repeating the movement of her head, either rubbing it on her front legs or wiping her muzzle with the paws, much as a cat does when washing its face. She would not touch food and could not lie still for five minutes; and we could do nothing to help her.

The Leopard and the Baboons

In spite of every care and effort we could not find out what was wrong with Jess, and she went through the night in suffering, making no sound, but moving from place to place weary and restless, giving long tired quivering sighs, and pawing at her mouth from time to time. In the morning light we again looked her all over carefully, and especially opened her mouth and examined her nostrils, but could find nothing to show what was wrong.

The puzzle was solved by accident. Ted was sitting on the ground when she came up to him, and looked wistfully into his face with a mute appeal for help.

'What is it, Jess, old girl?' he said, and reaching out, he caught her head in both hands and drew her towards him. Instantly with a sharp exclamation he let go again, pricked by something, and a drop of blood oozed from one fingertip. Under Jess's right ear there was a hard sharp point just showing through the skin. We all felt it, and when the skin was forced back we saw it was the tip of a porcupine quill. There was no pulling it out or moving it, however, nor could we for a long time find where it had entered. At last Ted noticed what looked like a tiny narrow strip of bark adhering to the outside of her lower lip, and this turned out to be the broken end of the quill, snapped off close to the flesh. Not even the end of the quill was visible — only the little strip that had peeled off in the breaking.

Poor old Jess! We had no very grand appliances for surgery, and had to slit her lip with an ordinary skinning knife. Ted held her between his knees and gripped her head with both hands, while one of us pulled with steel pliers on the broken quill until it came out. The quill had pierced her lower lip, entered the gums beside the front teeth, run all along the jaw and through the flesh behind, coming out just below the ear. It was over 17 centimetres long. She struggled a little under the rough treatment, and there was a protesting whimper when we tugged; but she did not let out one cry under all the pain.

We knew then that Jess had done her share in the fight, and guessed that it was she who in her reckless charge had rolled the porcupine over and given Jock his chance.

The doctoring of Jess had delayed us considerably and while we were still busy at it the old chief came up to say that his scouts had returned and reported that there was no leopard to be seen, but that they thought the trap had been sprung. They had not liked to go close up, preferring to observe the spot from a tree some way off.

The first question was what to do with Jess. We had no collar or chain, of course, and nothing would induce her to stay behind once Ted started. She would have bitten through ropes and reims in a few minutes, and no one would have faced the job of watching over and checking her. Finally we put her into one of the reed and mud huts, closed the entrance with some rawhides weighted with heavy stones, and off we went.

We found the trap sprung and the bait untouched. The spoor was a leopard's, right enough, and we saw where it had circled suspiciously all round before finally entering the little fenced approach which we had built to shepherd it on to the trap. There each footprint was clear, and it appeared that instead of cautiously creeping right up to

147

the bait and stepping on the setting-plate, it had made a pounce at the bait from about 3 metres away, releasing the trap by knocking the spring or by touching the plate with the barrel of its body. The leopard had evidently been nipped, but the body was too big for the teeth to close on, and no doubt the spring it gave on feeling the grip underneath set it free with nothing worse than a bad scraping and a tremendous fright. There was plenty of hair and some skin on the teeth of the trap, but very little blood there, and none at all to be found round about.

That was almost the worst result we could have had. The leopard was not crippled, nor was it wounded enough to enable us to track it, but it must have been so thoroughly alarmed that it would certainly be extremely nervous and suspicious of everything now, and would probably avoid the neighbourhood for some time to come.

The trap was clearly of no further use, but after coming so far for the leopard we were not disposed to give up the hunt without another effort. We were determined to go on, and if we failed to get a trace of the leopard, to put in the day hunting bushbuck or wild pig, both of which were fairly plentiful.

We had not gone more than a few hundred metres when an exclamation from one of the men made us look round, and we saw Jess on the opposite slope coming along full speed after us with her nose to the trail. She had scratched and bitten her way through the reed and mud wall of the hut, and raced away after us. She really did not seem much the worse for her wounds, and was — for her — quite demonstrative in her delight at finding us again.

In any case there was nothing to be done but to let her come, and we went on once more.

The guides led us into the woods where the big trees meeting overhead made it dark and cool. It was difficult in that light to see anything clearly, and the considerable undergrowth of shrub and creepers made progress slow. Although there did not seem to be much chance of finding the leopard at home, we crept along cautiously and noiselessly, talking — when we had to — only in whispers.

We were bunched together, preparing to crawl along a

rock overhanging a little pool, when the man in front made a sign and pointed with his assegai to the dogs. They had crossed the stream and were walking — very slowly and abreast — near the water's edge. The rawest of beginners would have needed no explanation. The two stood for a few seconds sniffing at a particular spot and then both together looked steadily upstream. There was another pause and they moved very slowly and carefully forward a metre or so and sniffed again with their noses almost touching. As they did this the hair on their backs and shoulders began to rise until, as they reached the head of the pool, they were bristling like hedgehogs and giving little purring growls.

The guide went over to them while we waited, afraid to move lest the noise of our boots on the stones should betray us. After looking round for a bit he pointed to a spot on the bank where he had found the fresh spoor of the leopard. There was no doubt about it then. The leopard had stopped to drink at the pool and probably to lick the scratches made by the trap; and leaving the bed of the stream it had gone through the thick undergrowth up towards the krans.

We were not more than a hundred metres from the krans then, and the track taken by the leopard was not at all an inviting one. It was at first merely a narrow tunnel in the undergrowth up the steep hillside, through which we crept in single file with the two dogs a few metres in front. They moved on in the same silent deliberate way, intent and strung up. As the ascent became steeper and more rocky, the undergrowth thinned, and we were able to spread out into line once more, threading our way through several roughly parallel game tracks or natural openings and stooping low to watch the dogs and take our cue from them.

We were about fifteen metres from the precipitous face of the krans, and had just worked round a huge boulder into a space fairly free of bush but cumbered with many big rocks and loose stones, when the dogs stopped. They stood quivering and bristling all over, moving their heads slowly about with noses well raised and sniffing persistently. There was something now that interested them more than the spoor; they winded the leopard itself, but could not tell where. No one stirred. We stood watching the dogs and snatching glances right and left among the boulders, and as we stood thus, grouped together in breathless silence, an electrifying snarling roar came from the krans above and the spotted body of the leopard shot like a streak out of the black mouth of a cave and across our front into the bush. There was a series of crashing bounds and then absolute silence.

We explored the den, but there was nothing of interest in it — no remains of food, no old bones, or other signs of cubs. It seemed to be the retreat of a male leopard — secluded, quiet and cool. The opening was not visible from any distance, a split-off slab of rock partly hiding it; but when we stood upon the rock platform we could see the kraal itself and the goats and cattle grazing on the slopes and in the valley below.

Leopards do not take their kill to their dens unless there are young cubs to be fed. As a rule they feed where they kill, or as near to it as safety permits, and when they have fed their fill they carry off the remainder of the carcass and hide it. Lions, hyenas, and others leave what they cannot eat and return to it for their next feed; but leopards are more provident and more cunning, and — being able to climb trees — they are very much more difficult to follow.

They are not big fellows, rarely exceeding two metres from nose to tip of tail and 60 kilograms in weight. But they are extraordinarily active and strong, and it is difficult to believe until one has seen the proof of it, that they are able to climb the bare trunk of a tree carrying a kill much bigger and heavier than themselves, and hang it safely wedged in some hidden fork out of reach of any other animal.

It would have been a waste of time to follow our leopard — he would be on the watch and on the move for hours. We gave it up at once, and struck across the spurs for another part of the big arena where pig and bushbuck were known to feed in the mornings.

We had nearly reached the kloof we were aiming for when we had the good luck to get a bushbuck in a very unexpected way. We had worked our way out of a particularly dense patch of bush and brambles into a corner of the woods and were resting on the mossy ground in the shade of the big trees when the sound of clattering stones a good way off made us start up again and grab our rifles. Presently we saw, outlined against the band of light which marked the edge of the timber, a buck charging down towards us. Three of us fired together, and the buck rolled over within a few metres of where we stood.

We were then in a 'dead end' up against the precipitous face of the Berg where there was no road or path other than game tracks, and where no human being ever went except for the purpose of hunting.

We knew there was no one else shooting there, and it puzzled us considerably to think what had scared the bushbuck; for the animal had certainly been startled. The pace, the noise it made, and the blind recklessness of its dash, all showed that. The only explanation we could think of was that the leopard, in making a circuit along the slopes of the Berg to get away from us, must have put the buck up and driven it down on to us in the woods below, and if that were so, the reports of our rifles must have made him think that he was never going to get rid of us.

We had failed to get the leopard, it is true, and it would be useless giving more time or further thought to him, but the porcupine had provided more interest and amusement than much bigger game might have done, and on the whole, although disappointed, we were not dissatisfied. In fact, it would have needed an ungrateful spirit indeed to feel discontented in such surroundings.

Big trees of many kinds and shapes united to make a canopy of leaves overhead through which only occasional shafts of sunlight struck. The cold mountain stream tumbling over ledges, swirling among rocks or rippling over pebble-strewn reaches, gurgled, splashed and bubbled with that

151

wonderful medley of sounds that go to make the lullaby of the brook. The floor of the forest was carpeted with a pile of staghorn moss 30 cm thick, and maidenhair fern grew everywhere with the luxuriant profusion of weeds in a tropical garden.

Long-tailed greeny-grey monkeys with black faces peered down at us, moving lightly on their branch trapezes, and pulled faces or chattered their indignant protest against intrusion. In the tops of the wild fig trees bright green pigeons watched us shyly. Gorgeous louries too flashed their colours and raised their crests, and beautiful little green-backed ruby-throated honey-suckers flitted like butterflies among the flowers on the sunlit fringe of the woods.

We stayed there until the afternoon sun had passed behind the crest of the Berg above us; and, instead of going back the way we came, skirted along the other arm enclosing the bay to have the cool shade of the mountain with us on our return journey.

Our route lay along the side of the spur, skirting the rocky backbone and winding between occasional boulders, clumps of trees and bush, and we had moved on only a little way when a loud 'waugh' from a baboon on the mountain behind made us stop to look back. The hoarse shout was repeated several times, and each time more loudly and emphatically. It seemed like the warning call of a sentry who had seen us. Moved by curiosity we turned aside on to the ridge itself, and from the top of a big rock scanned the almost precipitous face opposite.

The spur on which we stood was divided from the Berg itself only by a deep but narrow kloof or ravine, and every detail of the mountainside stood out in the clear evening air; but against the many-coloured rocks the grey figure of a baboon was not easy to find as long as it remained still, and although from time to time the barking roar was repeated, we were still scanning the opposite hill when one of the men pointed down the slope immediately below us and called out, 'There, there, Baas!'

The troop of baoons had evidently been quite close to us — hidden from us only by the little line of rocks — and on getting warning from their sentry on the mountain had stolen

quietly away and were then disappearing into the timbered
depth of the ravine. We sat still to watch them come out on
the opposite side a few minutes later and clamber up the
rocky face, for they are always worth watching. But while we
watched, the stillness was broken by an agonised scream
followed by roars, barks and bellows. The crackle of breaking
sticks and the rattle of stones added to the medley of sound
as the baboons raced out of the wood and up the bare rocky
slope.

'What is it?' 'What's the matter?' 'There's something
after them.' 'Look, look! There they come!' burst from
one and another of us as we watched the extraordinary
scene. The cries from below seemed to waken the whole
mountain. Great booming 'waughs' came from different
places far apart and ever so high up the face of the Berg.
Each big roar seemed to act like a trumpet call and bring
forth a multitude of others, and the air rang with bewildering shouts and echoes volleying round the kloofs and faces
of the Berg.

The strange thing was that the baboons did not continue
their terrified scramble up the mountain, but, once out of
the bush, they turned and rallied. Forming an irregular
semicircle they faced down hill, thrusting their heads forward
with sudden jerks as though to launch their cries with greater
vehemence. Feinting to charge they showered loose earth,
stones and debris of all sorts down with awkward underhand
scrapes of their fore-paws, and gradually but surely descend-

153

ed to within a dozen metres of the bush's edge.

'Baas, Baas, the leopard! Look, the leopard! There, there on the rock below!'

Jim shot the words out in vehement gusts, choky with excitement. True enough, there the leopard was. The long spotted body was crouched on a flat rock just below the baboons. He was broadside to us, with his fore-quarters slightly raised and his face turned towards the baboons. With wide-opened mouth he snarled savagely at the advancing line, and with right paw raised made threatening dabs in their direction. His left paw pinned down the body of a baboon.

The voices from the mountain boomed louder and nearer as, clattering and scrambling down the face, came more and more baboons. There must have been hundreds of them. The semicircle grew thicker and blacker, more and more threatening, metre by metre closer. The leopard raised himself a little more and took swift looks from side to side across the advancing front. Then his nerve went, and with one spring he shot from the rock into the bush.

There was an instant forward rush of the half-moon, and the rock was covered with roaring baboons, swarming over their rescued comrade. A moment later the crowd scrambled up the slope again, taking the leopard's victim with them. In that seething rabble I could pick out nothing, but others maintained they could see the mauled one dragged along by its arms by two others, much as a child might be helped uphill.

We were still looking excitedly about — trying to make out what the baboons were doing, when once more Jim's voice gave us a shock.

'Where are the dogs?' he asked, and the question turned us cold. If they had gone after the baboons they were as good as dead already — nothing could save them. Calling was useless. Nothing could be heard in the roar and din that the enraged animals still kept up. We watched the other side of the ravine with something more than anxiety, and when Jock's reddish-looking form broke through the bracken near to the leopard's rock, I felt like shutting my eyes till all was over. We saw him move close under the rock and then disappear. We watched for some seconds — it may have been a minute, but it seemed an eternity — and then, feeling the utter futility of waiting there, jumped off the rock and ran down the slope in the hope that the dogs would hear us call from there.

From where the slope was steepest we looked down into the bed of the stream at the bottom of the ravine, and the two dogs were there. They were moving cautiously down the wide stony watercourse just as we had seen them move in the morning, their noses thrown up and heads turning slowly from side to side. We knew what was coming. There was no time to reach them through the bush below. The cries of the baboons made calling useless, and the three of us sat down with rifles levelled ready to fire at the first sight. With gun gripped and breath hard held, watching intently every bush and tree and rock, every spot of light and shade, we sat — not daring to move.

Then, over the edge of a big rock overlooking the two dogs, appeared something round. Smoothly yet swiftly and with a snake-like movement, the long spotted body followed the head and, flattened against the rock, crept stealthily forward until the leopard looked straight down upon Jess and Jock.

The three rifles cracked like one, and with a howl of rage and pain the leopard shot out over the dogs' heads, raced along the stony bed, and suddenly plunging its nose into the ground, pitched over — dead.

It was shot through the heart, and down the ribs on each side were the scraped marks of the trap.

Buffalo, Bushfire and Wild Dogs

The summer slipped away. Among the massed evergreens of the woods there stood out here and there bright spots of colour. The careless dabs from Nature's artist hand; yellow and brown, orange and crimson, all vividly distinct, yet all in perfect harmony. The rivers, fed from the replenished mountains' stores, ran full and clear. The days were bright; the nights were cold; the grass was rank and seeding; and it was time to go.

Once more the bushveld beckoned us away.

We picked a spot where grass and water were good, and waited for the rivers to fall. It was while loitering there that a small hunting party from the fields making for the Sabi came across us and camped for the night. In the morning two of our party joined them for a few days to try for something big.

Two of us started out to try a new quarter in the hilly country rising towards the Berg. My companion, Francis, was an experienced hunter and his idea was that we would find the big game, higher up on the breezy hilltops or in the cool shady kloofs running towards the mountains. We passed a quantity of smaller game that morning, and several times heard the stampede of big animals — wildebeeste and water-

156

buck, as we found by the spoor — but it was absolutely impossible to see them. The dew was so heavy that even our hats were soaking wet, and times out of number we had to stop to wipe the water out of our eyes in order to see our way. A complete ducking would not have made the least difference.

Jock fared better than we did, finding openings and game tracks at his own level. He also knew better than we did what was going on ahead, and it was tantalising in the extreme to see him slow down and stand with his nose thrown up, giving quick soft sniffs and ranging his head from side to side, when he knew there was something quite close, and knew too that a few more toiling steps in that rank grass would be followed by a rush of something which we would never see.

After two hours of this we struck a stream, and there we made somewhat better pace and less noise, often taking to the bed of the creek for easier going. There, too, we found plenty of drinking places and plenty of fresh spoor of the bigger game, and as the hills began to rise in view above the bush and trees, we found what Francis was looking for. Something caught his eye on the far side of the stream, and he waded in. I followed and when half-way through saw the contented look on his face and caught his words: 'Buffalo! I thought so!'

We sat down then to think it out. The spoor told of a troop of a dozen to sixteen animals — bulls, cows and calves, and it was that morning's spoor. Even in the soft moist ground at the stream's edge the water had not yet oozed into

157

most of the prints. Fortunately there was a light breeze from the hills, and as it seemed probable that in any case they would make that way for the hot part of the day we decided to follow for some distance on the track and then make for the likeliest poort in the hills.

The buffalo had come up from the low country in the night on a course striking the creek diagonally in the drinking place. Their departing spoor went off a slight tangent from the stream — the two trails making a very wide angle at the drinking place and confirming the idea that after their night's feed in the rich grass lower down, they were making for the hills again in the morning and had touched at the stream to drink.

Jock seemed to gather from our whispered conversation and silent movements that there was work to hand, and his eyes moved from one face to the other as we talked. When we got up and began to move along the trail, he gave one of his little sideways bounds, as if he half-thought of throwing a somersault, and then with several approving waggings of his tail settled down at once to business.

Jock went in front. It was best so, and quite safe, for, whilst certain to spot anything long before we could, there was not the least risk of his rushing it or making any noise. The slightest whisper of a 'hst' from me would have brought him to a breathless standstill at any moment; but even this was not likely to be needed, for he kept a close watch on my face.

There was, of course, no difficulty whatever in following the spoor. The animals were as big as cattle, and their trail through the rank grass was as plain as a road. Our difficulty was to get near enough to see them without being heard. Under the downtrodden grass there were plenty of dry sticks to step on, any of which would have been as fatal to our chances as a pistol shot. Even the unavoidable rustle of the grass might betray us while the buffalo themselves remained hidden. Thus our progress was very slow.

We expected to follow the spoor for several kilometres before coming on the buffalo — probably right into the kloof towards which it appeared to lead — but were, nevertheless, quite prepared to drop on to them at any moment.

Jock moved steadily along the trodden track, sliding easily through the grass or jumping softly and noiselessly over impediments. We followed, looking ahead as far as the winding course of the trail permitted.

To right and left of us stood the screen of tall grass, bush and trees. Once Jock stopped, throwing up his nose, and stood for some seconds while we held our breath. But having satisfied himself that there was nothing of immediate consequence, he moved on.

I looked at Francis's face; it was pale and set like marble. His watchful grey eyes were large and wide, as though opened out to take in everything; and those moments of intense interest and expectation were the best part of a memorable day.

There was something near. We felt it. Jock was going more carefully than ever, with his head up most of the time. The feeling of expectation grew stronger and stronger until it amounted to absolute certainty. Then Jock stopped, stopped in mid-stride, not with his nose up ranging for scent, but with head erect, ears cocked, and tail poised — dead still. He was looking at something.

We had reached the end of the grass. Before us there was fairly thick bush mottled with black shadows and patches of bright sunlight in which it was most difficult to see anything. There we stood like statues, the dog in front with the two men abreast behind him, and all peering intently. Twice Jock slowly turned his head and looked into my eyes, and I felt keenly the sense of hopeless inferiority. 'There it is, what are you going to do?' was what the first look seemed to say; and the second: 'Well, what are you waiting for?'

How long we stood thus it is not possible to say; time is no measure of such things, and to me it seemed unending suspense; but we stood our ground scarcely breathing, knowing that something was there, because he saw it and told us so, and knowing that as soon as we moved it would be gone. Then close to the ground there was a movement — something swung, and the full picture flashed upon us. It was a buffalo calf standing in the shade of a big bush with its back towards us, and it was the swishing of the tail that had betrayed it. We dared not breathe a word or

159

pass a look — a face turned might have caught some glint of light and shown us up. So, we stood like statues each knowing that the other was looking for the herd and would fire when he got a chance at one of the full-grown animals.

My eyes were strained and burning from the intensity of the effort to see; but except the calf I could not make out a living thing. The glare of the yellow grass in which we stood and the sun-splotched darkness beyond it beat me.

At last, in the corner of my eye, I saw Francis's rifle rise, slowly. There was a long pause and then came the shot and wild snorts of alarm and rage. A dozen huge black forms started into life for a second and as quickly vanished — scattering and crashing through the jungle. The first clear impression was that of Jock, who after one swift run forward for a few metres stood looking back at me and waiting for the word to go. But at the sign of my raised hand, opened with palm towards him, he subsided slowly and lay down flat with his head resting on his paws.

'Did you see?' asked Francis.

'Not till you fired. I heard it strike. What was it?'

'Hanged if I know! I heard it too. It was one of the big 'uns, but bull or cow I don't know.'

'Where did you get it?'

'Well, I couldn't make out more than a black patch in the bush. It moved once, but I couldn't see how it was standing — end on or across. It may be hit anywhere. Expect he'll lay for us in the track somewhere.'

That is the way of the wounded buffalo — we all knew that, and old Rocky's advice came to mind with a good deal of point: 'Keep cool and shoot straight — or stay right home'; and Jock's expectant watchful look smote me with another memory — 'It was my dawg!'

A few metres from where the buffalo had stood we picked up the blood spoor. There was not very much of it, but we saw from the marks on the bushes here and there, and more distinctly on some grass further on, that the wound was pretty high up and on the right side. Crossing a small stretch of more open bush we reached the dense growth along the banks of the stream, and as this continued up into the kloof

160

it was clear we had a tough job before us.

Animals when badly wounded nearly always leave the herd and very often go downwind so as to be able to scent and avoid their pursuers. This fellow had followed the herd upwind, and that rather puzzled us.

A wounded buffalo in thick bush is considered to be about as nasty a customer as anyone may desire to tackle. Its vindictive indomitable courage and extraordinary cunning are a very formidable combination, as a long list of fatalities bears witness. Its favourite device — so old hunters will tell you — is to make off downwind when hit, and after going for some distance, come back again in a semicircle to intersect its own spoor, and there under good cover lie in wait for those who may follow up.

The huge black beast is able to hide itself so effectually that it can charge from a distance of a dozen metres on to those who are searching for it.

The secret of it seems to lie in two things. First, absolute stillness, and second, breaking up the colour. No wild animal, except those protected by distance and open country, will stand against a background of light or of uniform colour, nor will it as a rule allow its own shape to form an unbroken patch against its chosen background.

I have seen a wildebeest effectually hidden by a single blighted branch; a kudu bull by a few twisty sticks; a crouching lion by a wisp of feathery grass no higher than one's knee, no bigger than a vase of flowers. Yet the marvel of it is always fresh.

After a couple of hundred metres of that sort of going, we changed our plan, taking to the creek again and making occasional cross-cuts to the trail, to be sure he was still ahead. It was certain then that the buffalo was following the herd and making for the forge, so we took to the creek and made what pace we could to reach the narrow gorge where we reckoned to pick up the spoor again.

There are, however, few short cuts — and no certainties — in hunting. When we reached the poort there was no trace to be found of the wounded buffalo. The rest of the herd had passed in, but we failed to find blood or other trace of the wounded one, and Jock was clearly as much

161

at fault as we were.

We had overshot the mark and there was nothing for it but to hark back to the last blood spoor and by following it up, find out what had happened. This took over an hour, for we spoored him then with the utmost caution, being convinced that the buffalo, if not dead, was badly wounded and lying in wait for us.

We came on his 'stand', in a well-chosen spot, where the game path took a sharp turn round some heavy bushes. The buffalo had stood, not where one would naturally expect it — in the dense cover which seemed just suited for his purpose — but among lighter bush on the opposite side and about twenty metres nearer to us. There was no room for doubt about his hostile intentions. And when we recalled how we had instantly picked out the thick bush on the left as the spot to be watched, his selection of more open ground on the other side, and nearer to us, seemed so fiendishly clever that it made one feel cold and creepy. One hesitates to say it was deliberately planned; yet — plan, instinct or accident — there was the fact.

The marks showed us he was badly hit; but there was no limb broken, and no doubt he was good for some hours yet. We followed along the spoor, more cautiously than ever. On reaching the gorge, again we found his spoor, freshly made since we had been there. He had walked right along through the gorge without stopping again and gone into the kloof beyond.

Just before ascending the terrace we had heard the curious far-travelling sound of Blacks calling to each other from a distance, but, except for a passing comment, paid no heed to it, and passed on. Later we heard it again and, when we happened to pause in a more open portion of the bush after we had gone half-way along the terrace, the calling became so frequent and came from so many quarters that we stopped to take note. Francis, who spoke Zulu like one of themselves, at last made out a word or two which gave the clue.

'They're after the wounded buffalo!' he said.

Knowing that the buffalo was a long way ahead, we scrambled on as fast as we could whilst holding to his track. But it was very hot and very rough, and, to add to our troubles, smoke from a grass fire came driving into our faces.

Ten minutes later we stopped again. The smoke was perceptibly thicker; birds were flying past us downwind, with numbers of locusts and other insects. Two or three times we heard buck and other animals break back, and all were going the same way. Then the same thought struck us both — it was stamped in our faces. This was no ordinary mountain grass fire; it was a bush fire.

Francis was a quiet fellow, one of the sort it is well not to rouse. The blood rose slowly to his face, until it was bricky red, and he looked an ugly customer as he said, 'They have set the valley alight to burn him out. Come on quick. We must get out of this on to the slopes.'

We did not know then that there were no slopes, and after we had spent a quarter of an hour in that effort, we found our way blocked by the krans, and a tangle of undergrowth much worse than that in the middle of the terrace. The noise made by the wind in the trees and our struggling through the grass and bush had prevented our hearing the fire at first, but now its ever-growing roar drowned all sounds. Ordinarily, there would have been no real difficulty in avoiding a bush fire. But, pinned in between the river and the precipice and with kilometres of dense bush behind us, it was not at all pleasant.

Had we turned back even then and made for the gorge it is possible we might have travelled faster than the fire, but it would have been rough work indeed. Moreover, that would have been going back — and we did want to get the buffalo — so we decided to make one more try, towards the river this time. It was not much of a try, however, and we had gone no further than the middle of the terrace when it became alarmingly clear that this fire meant business.

The wind increased greatly, the air was thick with smoke, and full of flying things. In the bush and grass about us there was a constant scurrying. The terror of stampede was in the very atmosphere. A few words of consultation decided us, and we started to burn a patch for standing room and protection.

The hot sun and strong wind had long evaporated all

the dew and moisture from the grass, but the sap was still up, and our fire seemed cruelly long in catching on. With bunches of dry grass for brands we started burns in twenty places over a length of a hundred metres, and each little flame licked up, spread a little, and then hesitated or died out. It seemed as if our fire would never take, while the other came on with roars, leaps, and clouds of sparks and ash.

At last there was a fierce rush of wind and in a few seconds each little flame became a living demon of destruction. Another minute and the stretch before us was a field of swaying flame.

When we opened our scorched eyes the ground in front of us was all black, and on ahead, beyond the trellis work of bare scorched trees, the wall of flame swept on.

Then down on the wings of the wind came the other fire; and before it fled every living thing. A broken stream of terrified creatures dashed by, hardly swerving to avoid us. There is no coherent picture left of that scene — just a medley of impressions linked by flashes of unforgettable vividness.

A herd of kudu came crashing by. I know there was a herd, but only the first and last will come to mind, the space between seems blurred.

The wildebeest went by in indian file, uniform in shape, colour and horns, and strangely uniform in their mechanical action, lowered heads, and fiercely determined rush.

A rietbuck ram stopped close to us, looked back wide-eyed and anxious, whistled shrilly, and then cantered on with head erect and white tail flapping, but its mate neither answered nor came by. A terrified hare with its ears laid flat scuttled past within a metre of Francis and did not seem to

164

see him. Above us scared birds swept or fluttered downwind; while others came up swirling and swinging about, darting boldly through the smoke to catch the insects driven before the fire.

But what comes back with the suggestion of infinitely pathetic helplessness is the picture of a beetle. We stood on the edge of our burn, waiting for the ground to cool, and at my feet a pair of tock-tockie beetles, humpbacked and

bandy-legged, came toiling slowly and earnestly along. They reached the edge of our burn, touched the warm ash, and turned patiently aside — to walk round it!

There was one other thing seen, for a second or two only, but never to be forgotten. Out of the yellow grass came sailing down on us the swaying head and glittering eyes of a black mamba. The swiftest, most vicious, most deadly of snakes. Francis and I were not five metres apart and it passed between us, giving a quick chilly beady look at each — pitiless, and hateful. There was one hiss as the slithering tongue shot out and that was all. How much of the body was on the ground propelling it, I cannot even guess, but we had to look upwards to see the head as the snake passed between us.

The scorching breath of the fire drove us on to the baked ground, where we kept marking time to ease our blistering feet. Out hats were pulled down to screen our necks as we stood with our back to the coming flames. Our flannel shirts were so hot that we kept shifting our shoulders for relief. Jock, who had no screen and whose feet had no protection, was in my arms.

The heat was awful! Live brands were flying past all the

time, and some struck us. Myriads of sparks fell round and on us, burning numberless small holes in our clothing, and dotting blisters on our backs. Then, just at its maddest and fiercest there came a gasp and sob, and the fire died behind us as it reached the black bare ground. Our burn divided it as an island splits a flood, and it swept along our flanks in two great walls of living leaping roaring flame.

Two hundred metres away there was a bare yellow place in a world of inky black. The big bare antheap was untouched, and there we flung ourselves down, utterly done.

Faint from heat and exhaustion — scorched and blistered on face, arms, back and feet; weary and footsore, and with boots burnt through — we reached camp long after dark, glad to be alive.

We had forgotten the wounded buffalo. He seemed part of another life.

There was no more hunting for us. Our feet had 'gone in', and we were well content to sleep and rest. The burnt stubbly ends of the grass had pierced the baked leather of our boots many times, and Jock, too, had suffered badly and could hardly bear to set foot to the ground next day. The best we could hope for was to be sound enough to return to our own wagons in two or three days' time.

The camp was under a very large wild fig tree, whose dense canopy gave us shade all through the day. We had burnt the grass for some twenty or thirty metres round as a protection against bush fires, and as the trees and scrub were not thick just there it was possible to see in various directions rather further than one usually can in the bush-veld. The big tree was a fair landmark by day, and at night we made a good fire. These precautions were for the benefit of strayed or belated members of the party, but I mention them because the position of the camp and the fire brought us a strange visitor the last night of our stay there.

It was between eight and nine o'clock on the last day of our stay. Francis and I were fit again, and Jock's feet, thanks to care and washing and plenty of castor oil, no longer troubled him.

I was sitting on a small camp stool critically examining

166

my boots which had been resoled with rawhide in the rough but effective veld fashion, and Jock was lying in front of me when I saw his head switch up suddenly and his whole body set hard in a study of intense listening. He got up and trotted briskly off some ten or fifteen metres, and stood with his back towards me and his uneven ears topping him off.

I walked out to him, and silence fell on the camp. We all watched and listened. At first we heard nothing, but soon the call of a wild dog explained Jock's movements. The sound, however, did not come from the direction in which he was looking, but a good deal to the right, and as he instantly looked to this new quarter I concluded that this was not the dog he had previously heard. There was another wait, and then there followed calls from other quarters.

There was nothing unusual in the presence of wild dogs. Hyenas, jackals, wild dogs and all the smaller beasts of prey were heard nightly. What attracted attention in this case was the regular calling from different points. The wagon drivers said the wild dogs were hunting something and calling to each other so that those in front might turn the buck and by keeping it in a circle enable fresh or rested dogs to jump in from time to time and so, eventually, wear the poor hunted creature down. This is thought to be the system of the wild pack. When they cannot find easy prey in the young, weak or wounded, and are forced by hunger to hunt hard, they first scatter widely over the chosen area where game is located. One buck is then chosen — the easiest victim, a ewe with young for choice — and cutting it off from the herd, they follow that one and that one alone with remorseless invincible

167

persistency. There is something so hateful in the calculated pitiless method that one feels it a duty to kill the cruel brutes whenever a chance occurs.

The hunt went on round us. Sometimes it was near enough to hear the dogs' eager cries quite clearly, sometimes so far away that for a while nothing could be heard; and Jock moved from point to point in the circle of the fire's light so that he was always nearest to the chase.

At last hunters and hunted completed their wide circuit round the camp, and the end seemed near. There were no longer single calls widely separated, but the voices of the pack in hot close chase. They seemed to be passing a kilometre away from us. A few minutes more, and it was certain they were still nearer and coming straight towards us. We took our guns and I called Jock back to where we stood under the tree with our backs to the fire.

The hunt came at us like a cyclone out of the stillness, and in the forefront of it there burst into the circle of light an impala ewe with open mouth, haunting hunted despairing eyes, and widespread ears. The last staggering strides brought her in among us, tumbling at our feet.

The foremost of the pack followed hot foot close behind the buck — oblivious of fire and men, seeing nothing but the quarry — and at a distance of five metres a mixed volley of bullets and assegais tumbled it over. Another followed, and another. Both fell where they had stopped, a dozen metres away, puzzled by the fire and the shooting. Still more and more came on, but, warned by the unexpected check in front, they stopped at the clearing's edge, until over twenty pairs of eyes reflecting the fire's light shone out at us in a rough semicircle. The shot-guns came in better then, and more than half the pack went under that night before the others cleared off.

One of the wild dogs, wounded by a shot, seemed to go mad with agony and raced straight into the clearing towards the fire, uttering the strangest maniac-like yaps. Jock had all along been straining to go for them from where I had jammed him between my feet as I sat and fired, and the charge of this dog was more than he could bear. He shot out like a rocket and the collision sent the two flying apart. But he was on to

168

the wild dog again and had it by the throat before it could recover. Instantly the row of lights went out, as if switched off — they were no longer looking at us. There was a rustle and a sound of padded feet, and dim grey-looking forms gathered at the edge of the clearing nearest where Jock and the wounded dog fought. I shouted to Jock to come back, and several of us ran out to help.

It was an affair of a few seconds only for of course the instant we got a chance at the dog, without the risk of hitting Jock, we shot it and he, struggling to get at the others, was haled back to the tree.

While this was going on the impala stood with wide-spread legs, dazed and helpless, between Teddy Blacklow's feet. Its breath came in broken choking sobs; the look of terror and despair had not yet faded from the staring eyes; the head swayed from side to side; the mouth hung open and the tongue lolled out; all told beyond the power of words the tale of desperate struggle and exhaustion. It drank greedily from the dish that Teddy held for it — emptied it, and five minutes later drank it again and then lay down.

For half an hour it lay there, slowly recovering. At last it rose briskly, and standing between Teddy's knees looked about, taking no notice of his hands laid on either side and gently patting it. No one moved or spoke. Jock, at my feet, appeared most interested of all, but I am afraid his views differed considerably from ours on that occasion, and he must have been greatly puzzled. He remained watching intently with his head laid on his paws, his ears cocked, and his brown eyes fixed unblinkingly. At each movement on the buck's part something stirred in him, drawing every muscle tense and ready for the spring, but each time as I laid a hand on him he slackened out again and subsided.

We sat like statues as the impala walked out from its stall between Teddy's knees, and stood looking about wonderingly at the strange figures, and at the fire. It stepped out quite quietly, much as it might have moved about here and there any peaceful morning in its usual haunts. The head swung about briskly, but unalarmed, and ears and eyes were turned this way and that in easy confidence and mild curiosity.

It seemed to us like a scene in fairyland in which some spell held us while the beautiful wild thing strolled about unfrightened.

A few metres away it stopped for a couple of minutes with its back towards us and the fire. The silence was absolute. It stood thus with eyes and ears for the bush alone. There was a warning whisk of the white tail and it started off again — this time at a brisk trot — and we thought it had gone. But at the edge of the clearing it once more stood and listened. The ears flickered and the head turned slightly one way or another, but no sound came from the bush.

All was well.

It looked slowly round, giving one long full gaze back at us which seemed to be 'Goodbye, and — thank you', and cantered out into the dark.

Snowball and Tsetse

Snowball and Tsetse were horses; old soldiers who had seen the ups and downs of life. Like many old soldiers, Tsetse, who belonged to my friend Hall, was a stickler for etiquette and routine. For instance, he would not under any circumstances permit mounting on the wrong side — a most preposterous stand for an old salted shooting horse to take, and the cause of much inconvenience at times.

Snowball, who was my horse, had no unpractical prejudices: he objected to work — that was all. I bought him because he was 'salted' and would live in the bushveld. Beside that, all other considerations were trivial.

Hunting horses live almost entirely by grazing, as it is seldom possible to carry any grain or other foods for them. Salted horses have therefore a particular value in that they can be turned out to graze at night or in the morning and evening dews, when animals not immunised will contract horse sickness. Thus they feed during the hours when hunting is not possible and keep their condition when an unsalted horse would fall away from sheer want of food.

Of course he was said to be a shooting horse, and he took no notice of a gun fired under his nose or from his back — which was all the test I could apply at the time. His legs were quite sound; his feet were excellent; he had lost no teeth; and he was in tiptop condition. What more could one want? I did not know then that he was selfish, unscrupulous and a confirmed shirker.

171

Snowball had one disfigurement, consisting of a large black swelling as big as a small orange behind his left eye. It could easily have been removed, and many suggestions were made on the subject but all of them were firmly declined. Without that lump I should have had no chance against him. It was the weak spot in his defence, the only cover under which it was possible to stalk him when he made one of his determined attempts to avoid work. He could see nothing that came up behind him on the left side without turning his head completely round; hence one part of the country was always hidden from him, and of course it was from this quarter that we invariably made our approaches to attack.

So well did Snowball realise this that when the old villain intended giving trouble he would start off with his head swung away to the right, and when far enough away to graze in security, he would turn about and face towards the wagons. Keeping us well in view, he would either graze off sideways, or from time to time walk briskly off to occupy a new place, with the right eye swung round on us like a searchlight.

Against all this, however, it is only fair to admit that there were times when for days, and even weeks, at a stretch he would behave admirably, giving no more trouble than Jock did. Moreover he had qualities which were not to be despised. He was as sound as a bell, very clever on his feet, never lost his condition, and, although not fast, could last for ever at his own pace.

Experience taught me to take no chances with Snowball. He seemed to have moods — to get out of bed on the wrong side — on certain days and, for no reason in the world, behave with a calculated hostility that was simply maddening.

It was not, as a rule, at the outspan, where many hands were available, that Snowball gave trouble, but out hunting when I was alone or with only one companion. A trained shooting horse should stop as soon as his rider lays hand on mane to dismount, and should remain where he is until his master returns. Some horses require the reins to be dropped over their heads to remind them of their duty but many can safely be left to themselves and will be found

172

grazing quietly where left.

Snowball knew well what to do, but he pleased himself about doing it. Sometimes he would stand and sometimes he would move off a little way. Sometimes, with a troop of buck moving on ahead or perhaps a wounded one to follow, he would simply walk off with his ears laid back, his tail tucked down ominously, and occasional little liftings of his hindquarters to let me know what to expect.

To the credit of Snowball stand certain things, however, and it is but justice to say that, when once in the ranks, he played his part well. It is due to him to say that during one hard season a camp of wagons with their complement of men had to be kept in meat, and it was Snowball who carried — for short and long distances, through dry rough country, at all times of day and night, hot, thirsty, and tired, and without a breakdown or a day's sickness — a bag that totalled many thousands of kilograms in weight, and the man who made the bag.

On one long horseback journey through Swaziland to the coast, where few White men and no horses had yet been seen, we learned to know Snowball and Tsetse well, and found out what a horse can do when put to it. It was a curious experience on that trip to see whole villages flee in terror at the first sight of the new strange animals. In some places not even the grown men would approach, but too proud to show fear, they stood their ground, their bronze faces blanching visibly and setting hard as we rode up. Once, when we came unexpectedly upon a party of naked urchins playing on the banks of a stream, the whole pack set off full cry for the water and, jumping in like a school of alarmed frogs, disappeared. Infinitely amused by the stampede we rode up to see what had become of them, but the silence was absolute, and for a while they seemed to have vanished altogether. Then a tell-tale ripple gave the clue, and under the banks among the ferns and exposed roots we picked out little black faces half submerged and pairs of frightened eyes staring at us from all sides.

It is in the rivers that a man feels the importance of a good horse with a stout heart. When we crossed the Crocodile

173

River we chose the widest spot in the hope that it would be shallow and free of rocks. We fired some shots into the river to scare the crocodiles, and started to cross. But to our surprise Tsetse, the strong-nerved and reliable, who always had the post of honour in front, absolutely refused to enter.

The water of the Crocodile is at its best of amber clearness and we could not see bottom, but the sloping grassy bank promised well enough and no hint reached us of what the horses knew quite well. All we had was on our horses — food, blankets, billy, rifles and ammunition. We were off on a long trip and, to vary or supplement the game diet, carried a small packet of tea, a little sugar, flour, salt, and some beads with which to trade for fowls and thick milk. Thus there were certain things we could not afford to wet, and these we used to wrap in a mackintosh and carry high when it came to swimming; but this crossing looked so easy that it seemed sufficient to raise the packs instead of carrying them.

Tsetse, who in the ordinary way regarded the spur as part of the accepted discipline, resented it when there seemed to him to be sufficient reason. When Hall, astonished at Tsetse's unexpected obstinacy, gave him both heels, the old horse shot his encumbered rider off the raised pack, metres away on to the soft grass — water-bottle, rifle, bandolier and man landing in a lovely tangle.

174

I then put old Snowball at it, fully expecting trouble, but the old soldier was quite at home. He walked quietly to the edge, sat down comfortably, and slid into the water — launching himself with scarcely a ripple just like an old hippo. That gave us the explanation of Tsetse's tantrum. The water came up to the seat of my saddle and walking was only just possible. I stopped at once, waiting for Tsetse to follow, and Hall, prepared for another refusal, sat back and again used his spurs.

No doubt Tsetse, once he knew the depth, was quite satisfied and meant to go in quietly, and the prick of the spur must have been unexpected, for he gave a plunge forward, and Hall shot out overhead, landing half across Snowball's back. There was a moment of ludicrous but agonised suspense. Hall's legs were firmly gripping Tsetse behind the ears, while he sprawled on his stomach on Snowball's crupper, with the reins in one hand and the rifle in the other. Doubled up with suppressed laughter 1 grabbed a fistful of shirt and held on, expecting Tsetse to hoist his head or pull back and complete the disaster. But good old Tsetse never moved, and Hall, handing me the rifle, managed to swarm backwards on to Tsetse's withers and scramble on to the pack again.

Saddle-deep in the river — duckings and crocodiles forgotten — we sat looking at each other and laughed till we ached.

The river was about three hundred metres wide there with a good sandy bottom and of uniform depth, but, to our disappointment, we found that the other bank which had appeared to slope gently to the water's edge was in fact a sheer wall standing up two metres above the river level. The beautiful slope which we had seen consisted of water grass and reed tops. We tried a little way up and down, but found deeper water, mud and reeds, and no break in the bank. There seemed to be nothing for it but to go back again and try somewhere else.

Hall did not know how to give in, and he decided to have a shot at it.

Tsetse was ranged up beside the bank, and Hall standing in the saddle threw his rifle and bandolier up and then scrambled out himself. I then loosened Tsetse's girths from my seat on Snowball, and handed the packed saddle to Hall

who lay down on the bank to take it from me. We did the same with Snowball's load, including my own clothes, for, as it was already sundown, a ducking was not desirable.

I loosened one side of Tsetse's reins and threw the end up to Hall, and he handed me a long supple whip to stir Tsetse to his best endeavours. The water there was rather more than half saddle-flap high. I know that because it just left me a good expanse of hindquarters to aim at when the moment came.

'Now', yelled Hall, 'up, Tsetse. Up!' and whack went the stick. Tsetse reared up. He could not reach the top but struck his fore-feet into the moist bank near the top, and with a mighty plunge that soused Snowball and me, went out. The tug on the leading rein, on which Hall had thrown all his weight when Tsetse used it to lever himself up, had jerked Hall flat on his face, but he was up in a minute, and releasing Tsetse threw back the rein to get Snowball to face it while the example was fresh.

Then for the first time we thought of the crocodiles — and the river was full of them. But Snowball would never face that jump without someone behind him, and there was nothing for it but to fire some scaring shots, slip into the water, and get the job over as quickly as possible.

To our relief Snowball faced the jump quite readily. Indeed, the old sinner did it with much less effort and splash than the bigger Tsetse. But, in his anxiety to get me out, Hall rushed up to Snowball on the warty side and he got a scare and dragged Hall through the thorns, while I waited in the water for help.

What an age it seemed. Each reed shaken by the river breeze gave me goose-flesh and sent waves of cold shudders creeping over me. The cold smooth touch of a reed stem against my leg made me want to jump and to get out with one huge plunge as the horses had done.

Hall had to lie flat and reach his furthest to grip my hand, and I nearly pulled him in, scrambling up that bank like a chased cat up a tree.

When one comes to think it out, the bank must have been 3 metres high. It was mighty unpleasant, but it taught us what a horse can do when he puts his back into it.

Jock's Mistake

Half-way between the Crocodile and Komati rivers, there are half a dozen or more small kopjes between which lie broad richly grassed depressions, too wide and flat to be called valleys. There is no running water there in winter, but there are a few big pools — long narrow irregularly shaped bits of water — with shady trees around them.

I came upon the place by accident one day, and thereafter we kept it as our own preserve, for it was full of game, and a most delightful spot.

Apart from the discovery of this preserve, the day was memorable for the reason that it was my first experience of a big, mixed herd. I learnt that day how difficult the work may be when several kinds of game run together.

After a dry and warm morning the sight of the big pool had prompted an off-saddle. Snowball was tethered in a patch of good grass, and Jock and I were lying in the shade. When Jock began to sniff and walk upwind, I took the rifle and followed, and a little way off we came into dry vlei ground where there were few trees and the grass stood about waist high. Some two hundred metres away where the ground rose slightly and the bush became thicker there was a fair-sized troop of impala, perhaps a hundred or more, and just behind, and mostly to one side of them, were between twenty and thirty antelope.

We saw them clearly and in time to avoid exposing ourselves. They were neither feeding nor resting, but simply standing about, and individual animals were moving unconcernedly from time to time with an air of idle loitering. I tried to pick out a good antelope ram, but the impala were in the way, and it was necessary to crawl for some distance to reach cover.

Crawling in the bushveld is hard work and very rough on both hands and knees. Frequent rests are necessary; and in one of the pauses I heard a curious sound of soft padded feet jumping behind me. Looking quickly about I caught Jock in the act of taking his observations. The grass was too high for him to see over, even when he stood up on his hind legs, and he was giving jumps of slowly increasing strength to get the height which would enable him to see what was on.

I shall never forget that first view of Jock's ballooning observations. It became a regular practice afterwards, but it is that first view that remains a picture of him. I turned at the instant when he was at the top of his jump. His legs were all bunched up, his eyes staring eagerly and his ears had flapped out, giving him a look of comic astonishment. A sign with my hand brought him flat on the ground, looking distinctly guilty, and we moved along again, but I was shaking with silent laughter.

At the next stop I had a look back to see how he was behaving, and to my surprise, although he was following carefully close behind me, he was looking steadily away to our immediate right. I subsided gently on to my left side to see what it was that interested him, and to my delight

saw a troop of twenty to twenty-five blue wildebeest. They had evidently not seen us.

I worked myself cautiously round to face them so as to be able to pick my shot and take it kneeling, but whilst doing this I became conscious of something else looking at me. One hundred metres away, about half-way between the wildebeest and myself were a dozen zebra, all exactly alike, all looking full face at me. With their fore-feet together, their ears cocked, and their heads quite motionless they were gazing steadily at me, alive with interest and curiosity. There was something quite ludicrous in it, and something perplexing also. When I looked at the zebra the wildebeest seemed to get out of focus and were lost to me; when I looked at the wildebeest the zebra blurred and faded out of sight. The difference in distance, perhaps as much as the very marked difference in the distinctive colourings, threw me out, and the effect of being watched also told. Of course I wanted to get a wildebeest, but I was conscious of the watching zebra all the time, and, for the life of me, could not help constantly looking at them to see if they were going to start off and stampede the others.

Whilst trying to pick out the best of the wildebeest a movement away on the left made me look that way. The impala jumped off like one animal, scaring the antelope into a scattering rout. The zebra switched round and thundered off like a stampede of horses, and the wildebeest simply vanished. One signal in one troop had sent the whole lot off. Jock and I were left alone, still crouching, looking from side to side, staring at the slowly drifting dust, and listening to the distant dying sound of galloping feet.

It was a great disappointment, but the conviction that we had found a really good spot made some amends.

We made for the wagons along another route taking in some of the newly discovered country in the home sweep, and the promise of the morning was fulfilled. We had not been more than a few minutes on the way when a fine rietbuck ram jumped up within a dozen metres of Snowball's nose. Old Rocky had taught me to imitate the rietbuck's shrill whistle and this one fell to the first shot. He was a fine big fellow, and as Snowball put on airs and pretended to be nervous when it came to packing the meat, I had to blindfold him. I hoisted the buck up to a horizontal branch and lowered it on to his back.

Snowball was villainously slow and bad to lead. He knew that whilst being led neither whip nor spur could touch him, and when loaded up with meat he dragged along at a miserable walk.

We were labouring along in this fashion when we came on the wildebeest again. A White man on foot seems to be recognised as an enemy, but if accompanied by animals he may pass unnoticed for a long while. Attention seems to be fixed on the animals rather than the man, and frank curiosity instead of alarm is quite evidently the feeling aroused.

The wildebeest had allowed me to get close up. I picked out the big bull and took the shot kneeling, with my toe hooked in the reins to secure Snowball, taking the chance of being jerked off my aim rather than letting him go. But he behaved like an angel, and once more that day a single shot was enough.

Early next morning I set off to bring in the meat. There was very little wanton shooting with us, for when we had more fresh meat than was required, it was dried as 'biltong' for the days of shortage which were sure to come. By nine o'clock I was on my way eastwards along the line of the pools, not expecting much and least of all what fate had in store for Jock.

We passed the second pool, loitering a few minutes in the

181

cool shade of the evergreens to watch the green pigeons feeding on the wild figs, and then moved briskly into more open ground. It is not wise to step too suddenly out of the dark shade into strong glare, and it may have been that act of carelessness that enabled the kudu to get off before I saw them. They cantered away in a string with the cows in the rear. It was a running shot — end on — and the last of the troop, a big cow, gave a stumble, but catching herself up again she cantered off slowly.

There was no time for a second shot and we started off in hot pursuit. Fifty metres further on where there was a clear view I saw the kudu going no faster than an easy canter, and Jock was close behind.

Whether he believed there was a broken leg to grip, or was simply overbold, it is impossible to know. Whatever the reason, he jumped for one of the hind legs, and at the same moment the kudu lashed out viciously. One foot struck him under the jaw close to the throat, 'whipped' his head and neck back like a bent switch, and hurled him somersaulting backwards.

Jock lay limp and motionless, with the blood oozing from mouth, nose and eyes. I recollect feeling for his heart-beat and breath, shaking him roughly and calling him by name. Then, remembering the pool near by, I left him in the shade of a tree, filled my hat with water, and poured it over him. I poured it into his mouth, shaking him again to rouse him, and several times pressing his sides — bellows fashion — in a ridiculous effort to restore breathing.

The old hat was leaky and I had to grip the rough-cut ventilations to make it hold any water at all. I was returning with a second supply when with a great big heart-jump I saw Jock heel over from his side and with his forelegs flat on the ground raise himself to a resting position, his head wagging groggily and his eyes blinking in a very dazed way.

He took no notice when I called his name, but at the touch of my hand his ears moved up and the stumpy tail scraped feebly in the dead leaves. He was stone deaf, but I did not know it then. He lapped a little of the water, sneezed the blood away and licked his chops, and then, with evident effort, stood up.

182

But this is the picture which it is impossible to forget. The dog was so dazed and shaken that he reeled slightly, steadying himself by spreading his legs well apart, and there followed a few seconds' pause in which he stood thus. Then he began to walk forward with the uncertain staggery walk of a toddling child. His jaws were set close; his eyes were beady black, and he looked 'fight' all over. He took no notice of me, and I, never dreaming that he was after the kudu, watched the walk quicken to a laboured trot before I moved or called. But he paid no heed to the call. For the first time in his life there was rank open defiance of orders. Thinking he was maddened by the kick and not quite responsible for himself, and — more than that — admiring his pluck far too much to be angry, I ran to bring him back; but at a turn in his course he saw me coming, and this time he obeyed the call and signal instantly, and with a limp air of disappointment followed quietly back to the tree.

The reason for Jock's persistent disobedience that day was not even suspected then. I put everything down to the kick and he seemed to me to be 'all wrong', but indeed there was excuse enough for him. Nevertheless it was puzzling that at times he ignored me in a positively contemptuous fashion, and at others obeyed with all his old readiness. I neither knew he was deaf, nor realised that the habit of using certain signs and gestures when I spoke to him — and even of using them in place of orders when silence was imperative — had made him almost independent of the word of mouth. From that day he depended wholly upon signs, for he never heard another sound.

Jock came back with me and lay down; but he was not content. Presently he rose again and remained standing with his back to me, looking steadily in the direction taken by the kudu. It was fine to see the indomitable spirit, but I did not mean to let him try again. The kudu was as good as dead no doubt, yet a hundred kudu would not have tempted me to risk taking him out. To rest him and get him back to the camp was the only thought. I was feeling very soft about the dog then, and while I sat thus watching him and waiting for him to rest and recover, he started off again. But it was not as he had done before. This time he went with a spring and a rush, with head lowered and meaning business. In vain I called and followed. He outpaced me and left me in a few strides.

The kudu had gone along the right bank of the donga which, commencing just below the pool, extended a kilometre or more down the flat valley. Jock's rush was magnificent, but it was puzzling, and his direction was even more so, for he made straight for the donga.

I ran back for the rifle and followed. He had already disappeared down the steep bank of the donga when, through the trees on the opposite side, I saw a kudu cow moving along at a slow cramped walk. The donga was a deep one with perpendicular sides, and overhanging crumbling banks, and I reached it as Jock, slipping and struggling, worked his way up the other wall writhing and climbing through the tree roots exposed by the floods. As he rushed out the kudu saw him and turned. There was just a chance — a second of time, a metre of space — before he got in the line of fire; and I took it. One hind leg gave way, and in the short sidelong stagger that followed Jock jumped at the kudu's throat and they went down together.

It took me several minutes to get through the donga, and by that time the kudu was dead and Jock was standing, wide-mouthed and panting, on guard at its head. The second shot had been enough.

Jantje

There was no hunting for several days after the affair with the kudu cow. Jock looked worse the following day than he had done since recovering consciousness. His head and neck swelled up so that chewing was impossible and he could only lap a little soup or milk, and could hardly bend his neck at all.

On the morning of the second day Jim Makokel' came up with his hostile-looking swagger and a cross worried look on his face, and in a half-angry and wholly disgusted tone jerked out at me, 'The dog is deaf. I say so! Me! Makokela! Jock is deaf. He does not hear when you speak. Deaf! Yes, deaf!'

Jim's tone grew fiercer as he warmed up; he seemed to hold me responsible. The moment he spoke I knew it was true — it was the only possible explanation of many little things. Nevertheless I jumped up hurriedly to try him in a dozen ways, hoping to find that he could hear something. Jim was right. He was really stone deaf. It was pathetic to find how each little subterfuge that drew his eyes from me left him out of reach. It seemed as if a link had broken between us and I had lost my hold. That was wrong, however. In a few days he began to realise the loss of hearing, and after that, feeling so much greater dependence on sight, his watchfulness increased so that nothing escaped him. None of those who saw him in that year, when he was at his very best, could bring themselves to believe that he was deaf. With me it made differences both ways: something lost, and something gained. If he could hear nothing, he saw more. The language of signs developed, and taking it all round I believe the sense of mutual dependence and of mutual understanding was greater than ever.

There was a spot between the Komati and Crocodile rivers on the north side of the road where the White man seldom passed and nature was undisturbed. Few knew of water there; it was too well concealed between deep banks and the dense growth of thorns and large trees. The spot always had great attractions for me apart from the big game to be found there. I used to steal along the banks of this lone water and watch the smaller life of the bush. It was a delightful field for naturalist and artist.

There were numbers of little squirrel-like creatures; little fellows with bushy tails ringed in brown, black and white, of which the drivers made decorations for their slouch hats.

Along the water's edge one came on the lagavaans, huge repulsive water-lizards at least a metre long, like miniature crocodiles, sunning themselves in some favourite spot in the margin of the reeds or on the edge of the bank. They give one the jumps by the suddenness of their rush through the reeds and plunge into deep water.

There were otters, too, big black-brown fierce fellows, to be seen swimming silently close under the banks. I got a couple of them, but was always nervous of letting Jock into the water after things, as one never knew where the crocodile lurked.

There were certain hours of the day when it was more pleasant and profitable to lie in the shade and rest. If one remained quiet, there was generally something to see and something worth watching.

There were caterpillars clad in spiky armour made of tiny fragments of grass — fair defence no doubt against some enemies and a most marvellous disguise. Other caterpillars, clad in bark, were impossible to detect until they moved. There were grasshoppers like leaves, and irregularly shaped stick insects, with legs as bulky as the body, and all jointed by knots like irregular twigs — wonderful mimetic creatures.

Jock often found these things for me. Something would move and interest him, and when I saw him stand up and examine a thing at his feet, turning it over with his nose or giving it a scrape with his paw, it was usually worth joining in the inspection. The Hottentot gods always attracted him as they reared up and 'prayed' before him. Quaint things, with tiny heads, thin necks and enormous eyes, that sat up with forelegs raised to pray, as a pet dog sits up and begs.

One day I was watching the ants as they travelled along their route — sometimes stopping to hobnob with those they met, sometimes hurrying past, and sometimes turning as though sent back on a message or reminded of something forgotten — when a little dry brown bean lying in a spot of sunlight gave a jump of a few centimetres. At first it seemed that I must have unknowingly moved some twig or grass stem that flicked it. But as I watched it there was another vigorous jump. I took it up and examined it but there seemed nothing unusual about it. It was just a common light brown bean with no peculiarities or marks. It was a real puzzle, a most surprising and ridiculous one. I found half a dozen more in the same place, but it was some days before we discovered the secret. Domiciled in each of them was a very small but very energetic worm. A trapdoor or stopper was so artfully contrived on one end of the bean that it was almost impossible with the naked eye to locate

the spot where the hole was. The worm objected to too much heat and if the beans were placed in the sun or near the fire, the weird astonishing jumping would commence.

The beans were good for jumping for several months, and once in Delagoa, one of our party put some on a plate in the sun beside a fellow who had become a perfect nuisance to us. He had a mouthful of bread, and a mug of coffee on the way to help it down, when the first bean jumped. He gave a sort of peck, blinked several times to clear his eyes, and then pulled at his collar, as though to ease it. Then came another jump, and his mouth opened slowly and his eyes got big. The plate being hollow and glazed was not a fair field for the jumpers — they could not escape; and in about half a minute eight or ten beans were having a rough-and-tumble.

With a white scared face our guest slowly lowered his mug, got up and walked off without a word.

We tried to smother our laughter, but someone's choking made him look back and he saw the whole lot of us in various stages of convulsions. He made one rude remark, and went on, but everyone he met that day made some allusion to beans, and he took the Durban steamer next morning.

There is a goodness-knows-what-will-turn-up-next atmosphere about the bushveld which is, I fancy, unique. The story of the curate, armed with a butterfly net, coming face to face with a black-maned lion may or may not be true — in fact; but it is true enough as an illustration. It is no more absurd or unlikely than the meeting at five metres of a lioness and a fever-stricken lad carrying a white green-lined umbrella — which is true! The boy stood and looked. The lioness did the same. 'She seemed to think I was not worth eating, so she walked off', he used to say — and he was trooper 242 of the Imperial Light Horse who went back under fire for wounded comrades and was killed as he brought the last one out.

I knew an old cross-bred Hottentot-Bushman who half humorously and half seriously blended the folklore, stories and superstitions of his strange and dying race with his own hunting experiences.

Jantje had a wrinkled dry-leather face with hollow cheeks,

188

high cheek-bones, and little pinched eyes, so small and so deeply set that no one ever saw the colour of them. The peppercorns of tight wiry wool that did duty for hair were sparsely scattered over his head like the stunted bushes in the desert, and his face and head were seamed with scars too numerous to count.

I put Jantje on to wash clothes the day he turned up at the wagons to look for work, and as he knelt on the rocks stripped to the waist I noticed a very curious knotted line running up his right side from the lowest rib into the armpit.

He laughed almost hysterically, his eyes disappearing altogether and every tooth showing, as I lifted his arm to investigate the scar, and in high-pitched falsetto tones he shouted in a sort of ecstacy of delight, 'Die ou buffels, Baas! Die buffels bull, Baas!'

'Buffalo. Did he toss you?' I asked.

Jantje seemed to think it the best joke in the world and with constant squeals of laughter and graphic gestures gabbled off his account.

His master, it appears, had shot at and slightly wounded the buffalo, and Jantje had been placed at one exit from the bush to prevent the herd from breaking away. As they came towards him he fired at the foremost one, but before he could reload the wounded bull made for him and he ran for dear life to the only tree near — one of the flat-topped thorns. He heard the thundering hoofs and the snorting breath behind, but raced on hoping to reach the tree and dodge behind it. A few metres short, however, the bull caught him, in spite of a jump aside, and flung him with one toss right on top of the thorn tree.

When he recovered consciousness he was lying face upwards in the sun, with nothing to rest his head on and only sticks and thorns around him. He did not know where he was or what had happened. He tried to move, but one arm was useless and the effort made him slip and sag. He thought he was falling through the earth.

Presently he heard regular tramping underneath him and the breath of a big animal, and the whole incident came back to him. By feeling about cautiously he at last located the biggest branch under him, and getting a grip

189

on this he managed to turn over and ease his right side. He could then see the buffalo. It had tramped a circle round the tree and was doing sentry over him. Now and again the huge creature stopped to sniff, snort and stamp, and then resumed the round, perhaps the reverse way. The buffalo could not see him and never once looked up. Relying entirely on its sense of smell, it kept up the relentless vengeful watch for hours, always stopping in the same place, to leeward, to satisfy itself that the enemy had not escaped.

Late in the afternoon the buffalo, for the first time, suddenly came to a stand on the windward side of the tree. After a good minute's silence, it turned its tail on Jantje and with angry sniffs and tosses stepped swiftly and resolutely forward some paces. There was nothing to be seen, but Jantje judged the position and yelled out a warning to his master whom he guessed to be coming through the bush to look for him. At the same time he made what noise he could in the tree-top to make the buffalo think he was coming down. The animal looked round from time to time with swings and tosses of the head and threatening angry sneezes, much as one sees a cow do when standing between her young calf and threatened danger. It was defending Jantje, for his own purposes, and facing the danger.

For many minutes there was dead silence. No answer came to Jantje's call, and the bull stood its ground glaring and sniffing towards the bush. At last there was a heavy thud below, instantly followed by the report of the rifle — the bullet came faster than the sound. The buffalo gave a heavy plunge and with a grunting sob slid forward on its chest.

Round the camp fire at night Jantje used to tell tales in which fact, fancy, and superstition were curiously mingled. The drivers, for whose benefit they were told, listened open-mouthed, and I often stood at their fire, an interested listener.

The tale of his experiences with the honey bird which he had cheated of its share was the first I heard him tell. Who could say how much was fact, how much fancy, and how much the superstitions of his race? Not even Jantje knew that. He believed it all.

The honey bird met him one day with cheery cheep-cheep, and as he whistled in reply it led him to an old tree where the beehive was. It was a small hive, and Jantje was hungry, so he ate it all. All the time he was eating, the bird kept fluttering about, calling anxiously, and expecting some honey or fat young bees to be thrown out for it. When he had finished, the bird came down and searched in vain for its share. As he walked away the guilty Jantje noticed that the indignant bird followed him with angry cries and threats.

All day long he failed to find game. Whenever there seemed to be a chance an angry honey bird would appear ahead of him and cry a warning to the game. That night as he came back, empty-handed and hungry, all the portents of bad luck came to him in turn. An owl screeched three times over his head; a goatsucker with its long wavy wings and tail flitted before him in swoops and rings; a jackal trotted persistently in front looking back at him; and a striped hyena, humpbacked, savage, and solitary, stalked by in silence, and glared.

At night as he lay unable to sleep the bats came and made faces at him; a night adder rose up before his face and slithered out its forked tongue — the two black beady eyes glinting the firelight back; and whichever way he looked there was a honey bird, silent and angry, yet with a look of satisfaction, as it watched. So it went all night. No sleep for him. No rest!

In the morning he rose early and taking his gun and chopper set out in search of hives. He would give all to the honey bird he had cheated, and thus make amends.

191

He had not gone far before, to his great delight, there came a welcome chattering in answer to his low whistle, and the busy little fellow flew up to show himself and promptly led the way, going ahead ten to twenty metres at a flight. Jantje followed eagerly until they came to a small donga with a sandy bottom, and then the honey bird, calling briskly, fluttered from tree to tree on either bank, leading him on.

Jantje, thinking the hive must be near by, was walking slowly along the sandy bed and looking upwards in the trees when something on the ground caught his eye and he sprang back just as the head of a big puff-adder struck where his bare foot had been a moment before. With one swing of his chopper he killed it. He took the skin off for an ornament, the poison glands for medicine, and the fangs for charms, and then whistled and looked about for the honey bird, but it had gone.

A little later on, however, he came upon another, and it led him to a big and shady wild fig tree. The honeybird flew to the trunk itself and cheeped and chattered there, and Jantje put down his gun and looked about for an easy place to climb. As he peered through the foliage he met a pair of large green eyes looking full into his. On a big limb of the tree lay a leopard, still as death, with its head resting on its paws, watching him with a cat-like eagerness for its prey. Jantje hooked his toe in the reim sling of his old gun and slowly gathered it up without moving his eyes from the leopard's, and backing away slowly, step by step, he got out into the sunshine and made off as fast as he could.

It was the honey bird's revenge. He knew it then.

He sat down on some bare ground to think what next to do, for he knew he must die if he did not find honey and make good a hundred times what he had cheated.

All day long he kept meeting honey birds and following them. But he would no longer follow them into the bad places, for he could not tell whether they were new birds or the one he had robbed. Once he had nearly been caught. The bird had perched on an old antheap, and Jantje, thinking there was a ground hive there, walked boldly forward. A small misshapen tree grew out of the antheap, and one of the twisted branches caught his eye because of the thick ring around it. It was the coil of a long green mamba, and far below that, half-hidden by the leaves, hung the snake's head with the neck gathered in half-loop coils ready to strike him.

After that Jantje kept in the open, searching himself among rocks and in old dead trees for the tell-tale stains that mark the hive's entrance. But he had no luck, and when he reached the river in the early afternoon he was glad of a cool drink and a place to rest.

For a couple of hours he had seen no honey birds, and it seemed that at last his pursuer had given him up, for that day at least. As he sat in the shade of the high bank, however, with the river only a few metres from his feet, he heard again a faint chattering. It came from the riverside beyond a turn in the bank, and it was too far away for the bird to have seen Jantje from where it called, so he had no doubt about this being a new bird. It seemed to him a glorious piece of luck that he should find honey by the aid of a strange bird, and be able to take half of it back to the hive he had emptied the day before and leave it there for the cheated bird.

There was a beach of pebbles and rocks between the high bank and the river, and as Jantje walked along it on the keen look-out for the bird, he spotted it sitting on a root half-way down the bank some twenty metres ahead. Close to where the chattering bird perched there was a break in the pebbly beach, and there shallow water extended up to the perpendicular bank. In the middle of this little stretch of water, and conveniently placed as a stepping-stone, there was a black rock, and the barefooted Jantje stepped noiselessly from stone to stone towards it.

An alarmed cane rat, cut off by Jantje from the river, ran along the foot of the bank to avoid him, but when it reached the little patch of shallow water it suddenly doubled back in fright and raced under the boy's feet into the river.

Jantje stopped. He did not know why, but there seemed to be something wrong. Something had frightened the cane rat back to him, and he stared hard at the bank and the stretch of beach ahead of him. Then the rock he meant to step on to gave a heave, and a long blackish thing curved towards

193

him; he sprang into the air as high as he could, and the crocodile's tail swept under his feet.

Jantje fled back like a buck — the rattle on the stones behind him and crash of reeds putting metres into every bound.

For four days he stayed in camp waiting for someone to find a hive and give him honey enough to make his peace. Then, for an old snuff box and a little powder, he bought a huge basketful of comb, and put it all at the foot of the tree he had cleaned out.

Then he had peace.

The men believed every word of that story: so, I am sure, did Jantje himself. The buffalo story was obviously true, and Jantje thought nothing of it. The honey bird story was not, yet he gloried in it. It touched his superstitious nature, and it was impossible for him to tell the truth or to separate fact from fancy and superstition.

How much of fact there may have been in it I cannot say. Honey birds gave me many a wild-goose chase, but when they led to anything at all it was to hives, and not to snakes, leopards and crocodiles. Perhaps it is right to own up that I never cheated a honey bird. We pretended to laugh at the superstition, but we left some honey all the same — just for luck. After all, as we used to say, the bird earned its share and deserved encouragement.

Monkeys and Wildebeest

Mungo was not a perfect horse, but he was a great improvement on Snowball, who had gone on to the retired list soon after Jock became deaf. He had a wretched walk, and led almost as badly as his predecessor, but this did not matter so much because he could be driven like a pack donkey and relied on not to play pranks. In a gallop after game he was much faster than Snowball, having a wonderfully long stride for so low a pony.

Sometimes after a long night's trekking I would start off after breakfast for some 'likely' spot, off-saddle there in a shady place, sleep during the heat of the day, and after a billy of tea start hunting towards the wagons in the afternoon.

It was in such a spot on the Komati River, a couple of hundred metres from the bank, that on one occasion I settled down to make up lost ground in the matter of sleep. With Mungo knee-haltered in good grass and Jock beside me, I lay flat on my back with my hat covering my eyes and was soon comfortably asleep.

The sleep had lasted a couple of hours when I began to dream that it was raining and woke up in the belief that a hailstorm — following the rain — was just breaking over me. I started up to find all just as it had been, and the sunlight beyond the big tree so glaring as to make the eyes ache.

195

Through half-closed lids I saw Mungo lying down sleeping and made out Jock standing some metres away quietly watching me.

With a yawn and stretch I lay back again; sleep was over but a good lazy rest was welcome. It had been earned, and, most comforting of all, there was nothing else to be done. In the doze that followed I was surprised to feel quite distinctly something like a drop of rain strike my leg, and then another on my hat.

'Hang it all, it is raining', I said, sitting up again and quite wide awake this time. There was Jock still looking at me, but a minute later he looked up into the tree above me with ears cocked, head on one side, and tail held lazily on the horizontal and moving slowly from time to time.

It was his look of interested amusement.

A couple of leaves fluttered down, and then the half-eaten pip of a 'wooden orange' struck me in the face as I lay back again to see what was going on above. The pip gave me the line, and away up among the thick dark foliage I saw a little old face looking down at me. The quick restless eyes were watchfully on the move, the face and attitude together a vivid expression of surprise, indignation and breathless interest.

As my eyes fairly met those above me, the monkey ducked its head forward and promptly 'made a face' at me without uttering a sound. Then others showed up in different places, and whole figures became visible now as the monkeys stole softly along the branches to get a better look at Jock and me. There were a couple of dozen of them of all sizes.

They are the liveliest, most restless, and most inquisitive of creatures. Ludicrously nervous and excitable they are quick to chattering anger and bursts of hysterical passion, which are intensely comical, especially when they have been scared. They are creatures whose method of progress most readily betrays them by the swaying of a branch or quivering of leaves, yet they can steal about and melt away at will, like small grey ghosts.

I had often tried to trap them, but never succeeded. Jantje caught them, but he disliked showing his traps, and when told to explain he would half-sulkily show one of the common kind.

The day he caught the monkey he was well pleased, and may possibly have told the truth. Baboons and monkeys, he said, can count just like men, but they can only count two. If one man goes into a mealie field and waits for them with a gun, their sentry will see him, and he may wait for ever. If two go and one remains, it is useless, for they realise that only one has come out where two went in. But if three go in, one may remain behind to lie in wait for them, for the monkeys, seeing more than one return, will invade the mealie field as soon as the two are safely out of the way. That was only Jantje's explanation of the well-known fact that monkeys and baboons know the difference between one and more than one.

But, as Jantje explained, their cleverness helped him to catch them. He went alone and came away alone, leaving his trap behind, knowing that they were watching his every movement, but knowing also that their intense curiosity would draw them to it the moment it seemed safe. The trap he used was an old calabash or gourd with a round hole in it 9 centemetres in diameter. A few pumpkin seeds and mealies and a hard crust of bread, just small enough to get into the calabash, formed the bait.

After fastening the gourd by a cord to a small stump, he left it lying on its side on the ground where he had been sitting. A few crumbs and seeds were dropped near it and the rest placed in the gourd, with one or two showing in the mouth. Then he walked off on the side where he would be longest in view, and when well out of sight sped round in a circuit to a previously selected spot where he could get close up again and watch.

The foremost monkey was already on the ground when he got back and others were hanging from low branches or clinging to the stems, ready to drop or retreat.

After a pause they began the careful roundabout approach and the squatting and waiting, making pretences of not being particularly interested, while their quick eyes watched everything; then the deft picking up of one thing — instantly dropped again, as one picks up a roasted chestnut and drops it in the same movement, in case it should be hot; and finally the greedy scramble and chatter.

Jantje waited until the tugs at the gourd became serious, and then, knowing that the smaller things had been taken out or shaken out and eaten and that some enterprising monkey had put its arm into the hole and grabbed the crust, he ran out.

A monkey rarely lets go any food it has grabbed, and when, as in this case, the hand is jammed in a narrow neck, the act requires a deliberate effort. So Jantje caught his monkey, and flinging his ragged coat over the captive sat down to make it safe.

By pushing the monkey's arm deeper into the gourd the crust became released and the hand freed. He then gradually shifted the monkey about until he got the head into the shoulders of the loose old coat, and thence into the sleeve. He had the creature as helpless as a mummy with the head appearing at the cuff opening and the body jammed in the sleeve like a bulging overstuffed sausage. The monkey struggled, screamed, chattered, made faces, and cried like a child; but Jantje gripping it between his knees was unmoved.

He next took the cord from the calabash and tied one

end securely round the monkey's neck and tied the other end to a stout bush stick about two or three metres long. Then he slipped monkey, cord and stick back through the sleeve and had his captive safe. The cord prevented it from getting away, and the stick prevented it from getting too close and biting him.

The grimacing little imps invariably tempt one to tease or chase them, just to see their antics and methods. When I rose, openly watching them and stepping about for a better view, they abandoned the silent method and bounded freely from branch to branch for fresh cover, always ducking behind something if I pointed the gun or a stick at them, and getting into paroxysms of rage and leaning over to slang and cheek me whenever it seemed safe.

Jock was full of excitement, thoroughly warmed up and anxious to be at them, running about from place to place to watch them, tacking and turning and jumping for better views. Now and then he ran to the trunk and scraped at it. Whenever he did this there was a moment's silence. The idea of playing a trick on them struck me and I caught Jock up and put him in the fork of a big main branch about 2 metres from the ground. The effect was magical. The whole of the top of the tree seemed to whip and rustle at once, and in two seconds there was not a monkey left.

Then a wave in the top of a small tree some distance off betrayed them and we gave chase — a useless romping schoolboy chase. They were in the small trees away from the river and it was easy to see and follow them. To add to the fun and excitement I threw stones at the branches behind them. Their excitement and alarm then became hysterical, and as we darted about to head them off they were several times obliged to scamper a few metres along the ground to avoid me and gain other trees. It was then that Jock enjoyed himself most. He ran at them and made flying leaps and snaps as they sprang up into the trees and out of reach. They finally got away into the big trees once more, to Jock's disappointment but greatly to my relief, for I was quite pumped from the romp and laughter.

The river at this point was broken into several sluices by islands formed of piles of rocks on which there were a few stunted trees and dense growths of tall reeds, and here and there little spits and fringes of white sand were visible. There was plenty of small game in that part, but half an hour's jogging along the bank having failed to propose anything, I struck away from the river taking a line through the bush towards camp, and eventually came across a small herd of blue wildebeest. Mungo's pricked ears and raised head warned me, but the grass being high it was not easy to see enough of them from the ground to place an effective shot, and before a chance offered they moved off slowly. I walked after them, leading Mungo and trying to get a fair opening on slightly higher ground.

Presently half a dozen blackish things appeared above the tall grass. They were the heads of the wildebeest — all turned one way, and all looking at us with ears wide-spread. Only the upper halves of the heads were visible through the thinner tops of the grass, and an ordinary standing shot was not possible. I had to go to a tree for support in order to tiptoe for the shot, and whilst in the act of raising my rifle the heads disappeared, but I took a chance and fired just below where the last one had shown up.

The wildebeest were out of sight, hidden by grass two metres high, but a branch of the tree beside me served as a horizontal bar and hoisting myself chin high I was able to see them again. In front of us there was a dry vlei quite free of bush, and the wildebeest had gone away to the right and were skirting the vlei, apparently meaning to get round to the opposite side, avoiding the direct cut across the vlei for reasons of their own. It occurred to me that there must be a deep donga or perhaps a mud hole in front which they were avoiding; but that it might be possible for me to get across, in time to have another shot at them the next time they stopped to look back. So I ran straight on.

One does not reason things out like that in practice.

The conclusion comes instantly, as if by instinct, and no time is lost. To drop from the branch, pick up the rifle, and start running were all part of one movement. Stooping slightly to prevent my bobbing hat from showing up in the grass tops, and holding the rifle obliquely before me as a sort of snow-plough to clear the grass from my eyes, I made as good pace as the ground would allow.

No doubt the rifle held in front of me made it difficult to notice anything on the ground, but the concentrated stare across the vlei in the direction of the galloping wilde-beest was quite as much the cause of what followed.

Going fast and stooping low, with all my weight thrown forward, I ran right into a wildebeest cow. My shot had wounded her through the kidneys, completely paralysing the hindquarters, and she had instantly dropped out of sight in the grass. The only warning I got was a furious snort, and the black-looking monster with great blazing bloodshot eyes rose up on its front legs as I ran into it.

To charge into a wounded wildebeest ready to go for you, just when your whole attention is concentrated upon others two hundred metres beyond, is nearly as unpleasant as it is unexpected. It becomes a question of what will happen to you, rather than of what you will do. That at any rate was my experience. The rifle, if it had hindered me, also helped. Held out at arm's length it struck the wildebeest across the forehead and the collision saved my chest from the horns. There was an angry toss of the big head and the rifle was twirled out of my hand, as one might flip a match away.

I do not know exactly what happened. The impression is of a breathless second's whirl and scramble, and then finding myself standing untouched five metres away.

The rifle lay within the circle of the wildebeest's big hooked horns, and the squatting animal, making a pivot of its hindquarters, slewed round and round, making savage lunges at Jock — who had intervened to help me — and great heaves at me each time I tried to get the rifle.

I tried to hook the gun out with a stick but the wilde-beest swung round and faced me at once, snapping the sticks and twirling them out of my hands with surprising ease and quickness. I then tried another game, and by making feint

attacks from the other side at last got the animal gradually worked away from my gun. The next attempt at raking was successful.

When the excitement was over and there was a chance of taking stock of the position, I found that Jock had a pretty good 'gravel rash' on one hip and a nasty cut down one leg. He had caught the wildebeest by the nose the instant I ran into it, and it had 'wiped the floor' with him and flung him aside.

I found my bandolier with a broken buckle lying on the grass. One shirt sleeve was ripped open and the back of my right hand cut across. My hands and knees were well grated and there were lumps and bruises about the legs for which there was no satisfactory explanation. I must have scrambled out like an unwilling participant in a dog fight.

It was a long job skinning, cutting up, and packing the wildebeest, and when we reached the outspan the wagons had already started and we had a long tramp before us to catch them.

I drove Mungo before me, keeping him at an easy jog. We had been going for possibly an hour and it was quite dark, except for the stars and the young moon low down on our right. The road was soft and Mungo's jogging paces sounded like floppy pats. There was no other sound at all, not even a distant rumble from the wagons to cheer us. Mungo must have been sick of it and one might have thought him jogging in his sleep but for the occasional pricking of his ears — a trick that always makes me wonder how much more horses see in the dark than we do. I walked like a machine, with my rifle on my shoulder, glad to be rid of the broken bandolier, then transferred to Mungo; and Jock trotted at my heels.

This tired monotonous progress was undisturbed until Mungo stopped. His ears pricked, his head went up, and he looked hard at a big low bush on our left. I gave him a tap with the switch, and without hesitation he dashed off to the right, made a half-circle through the veld, came into the road fifty metres ahead, and galloped away leaving a rising column of dust behind him.

Then Jock growled low and moved a few steps forward and slightly to the right, also sheering off from that bush. I felt that he was bristling all over, but there was neither time nor light to watch him. I stepped slowly sideways after him, gripping the rifle and looking hard at the bush.

Our line was much the same as Mungo's and would take us some seven or eight paces off the road — more than that was not possible owing to the barrier of thorns on that side. When we got abreast of the bush two large spots of pale light appeared in the middle of it, waist high from the ground.

It is impossible to forget the tense creepy feeling caused by the dead stillness, the soft light, and the pale expressionless glow of those eyes — the haunting mystery of eyes and nothing more.

It is not unusual to see eyes in the night, but this was a 'nervy' occasion, and there is no other that comes back with all the vividness and reality of the experience itself, as this one does.

As we moved on and passed the reflecting angle of the moon, the light of the eyes went out as suddenly and silently as it had appeared. There was nothing then to show me where danger lay, but Jock knew, and I kept a watch on him. He jogged beside me, lagging slightly as if to cover our retreat, always looking back. A couple of times he stopped entirely

203

and stood in the road, facing straight back and growling, and I followed suit. He knew that he was in command.

There was nothing more. Gradually Jock's subdued purring growl died down and the glances back became fewer. I found Mungo a long way on, brought to a standstill by the slipping of his load; and we caught up to the wagons at the next outspan.

The Old Crocodile

We reached the Crocodile River drift on a Sunday morning after a particularly dry and dusty night trek. 'Wanting a wash' did not on such occasions mean a mild inclination for a luxury. It meant that washing was badly needed. The dust lay very deep on the worn veld road, and the long strings of oxen toiling along kicked up suffocating clouds of fine dust which powdered White man and Black to an equal level of yellowy red. The wagons were a couple f hundred metres from the river, and, taking a complete change, I went off for a real clean up.

We generally managed to get in a couple of real swims, but that was only done in the regular drifts and when there were people about or wagons crossing. In such conditions crocodiles rarely appear. They prefer solitude and silence.

Being alone that day I had no intention of having a swim or of going into the open river, and I took a little trouble to pick a suitable pool with a rock on which to stand and wash. The water was clear and I could see the bottom of the pool. It was quite shallow — one metre deep at most and divided from the main stream by a narrow spit of sand. At the top end of the sand spit was a flat rock — my dressing-table.

After a dip in the pool I stood on the sand spit to scrub

off the brown dust, keeping one unsoaped eye roving round for intrusive crocodiles, the loaded rifle lying beside me. The brutes slide out so silently and unexpectedly that in that exposed position, with water all round, one could not afford to turn one's back on any quarter for long. There is something laughable — it seemed faintly humorous even then — in the idea of a naked man hastily washing soap out of his eyes and squeezing away the water to take a hurried look behind him, and then after careful survey, doing an 'altogether' dowse just as hastily — blowing and spluttering all the time like a boy after his first dive.

The bath was successful and ended without incident — not a sign of a crocodile the whole time. Breakfast was ready when I reached the wagons, and feeling very fit and clean in a fresh flannel shirt and white moleskins, I sat down to it. Jim Makokel' brought the kettle of coffee from the fire and was in the act of pouring some into a big mug when he stopped with a grunt of surprise and, looking towards the river, called out sharply, 'What is it?'

One of the herdsmen was coming at a trot towards us, and the drivers, thinking something had happened to the oxen, called a question to him. He did not answer until he reached them and even then spoke in so quiet a tone that I could not catch what he said. But Jim, putting down the kettle, ran to his wagon and, grabbing his sticks and assegais, called to me in a husky shouting whisper: 'Ingwenye, Inkos. Ingwenye, Umkulu. Big Clocodile. Groot Krokodil, Baas!'

Then abandoning his excited polyglot he gabbled off in pure Zulu and at incredible speed a long account of the big crocodile. It had carried off four miners going to the gold-fields that year. It had taken a woman and a baby from the kraal near by, but a White man had beaten it off with a bucket. It had taken all the dogs, and even calves and goats, at the drinking place, and goodness knows how much more. How Jim got his news, and when he made his friends, were puzzles never solved.

I took the rifle and went with the herdsman. Jim followed close behind, walking on his toes with the waltzy springy movement of an ostrich, eager to get ahead and repeatedly silenced and driven back by me in a few hundred metres, walk

206

to the river.

A queer premonitory feeling came over me as I saw we were making straight for the bathing pool, but before reaching the bank the herdsman squatted down, indicating that somewhere in front and below us the enemy would be found. An easy crawl brought me to the river bank and, sure enough, on the very spot where I had stood to wash, only fifty metres from us, there was an enormous crocodile. He was lying along the sand spit with his full length exposed to me. Such a shot should have been a moral certainty, but as I brought the rifle slowly up it may have glinted in the sun, or perhaps the crocodile had been watching us all the time, for with one easy turn and no splash at all he slid into the river and was gone.

It was disgusting and I pitched into Jim and the others for having made a noise and shown themselves, but they were still squatting when I reached them and vowed they had neither moved nor spoken. We had already turned to go when there came a distant call from beyond the river. To me it was quite meaningless, but to Jim's trained ears it spoke clearly. Jim pressed me downwards and we all squatted again.

'He is coming out on another sandbank', Jim explained.

Again I crawled to the bank and lay flat, with the rifle ready. There was another sand streak a hundred metres out in the stream with two outcroppings of black rock at the upper end of it — they were rocks right enough, for I had examined them carefully when bathing. This was

the only other sandbank in sight. It was higher than it appeared to be from a distance and the crocodile whilst hidden from us was visible to the Blacks on the opposite bank as it lay in the shallow water and emerged bit by bit to resume its morning sunbath.

The crocodile was so slow in showing up that I quite thought it had been scared off again, and I turned to examine other objects and spots up and down the stream. But presently glancing back at the bank again I saw what appeared to be a third rock, no bigger than a loaf of bread. This object I watched until my eyes ached and swam. It was the only possible crocodile, yet it was so small, so motionless, so permanent looking, it seemed absurd to doubt that it really was a stone which had passed unnoticed before.

As I watched unblinkingly it seemed as if it swelled and shrank with breathing, and knowing that this must be merely an optical illusion caused by staring too long, I shut my eyes for a minute. The effect was excellent. The rock was much bigger, and after that it was easy to lie still and wait for the cunning old reptile to show himself.

It took half an hour of this cautious manoeuvring and edging on the part of the crocodile before he was comfortably settled on the sand with the sun warming his back. In the meantime the wagon drivers behind me had not stirred. On the opposite side of the river men, women and children from the neighbouring kraal had gathered to the number of thirty or forty, and they stood loosely grouped, instinctively still, silent and watchful, like a little scattered herd of deer. All on both sides were watching me and waiting for the shot. It seemed useless to delay longer. The whole length of the body was showing, it was evident that the crocodile was lying, not on the top, but on the opposite slope of the sand spit, and probably not more than fifteen centimetres — in depth — of body was visible.

It was little enough to aim at, and the bullet seemed to strike the top of the bank first, sending up a column of sand, and then, probably knocked all out of shape, it ploughed into the body with a tremendous thump.

The crocodile threw a back somersault — that is, it seemed to rear up on its tail and spring backwards. The jaws divided

into a huge fork as, for a second, it stood up on end, and let out an enraged roar. It had a very sudden and dramatic effect, following on the long silence.

Then the whole world seemed to burst into indescribable turmoil. Shouts and yells burst out on all sides. The men armed with sticks and assegais rushed down to the banks and the women and children followed armed with nothing more formidable than their voices. The crocodile was alive — very much alive — and in the water. The wagon drivers, headed by Jim, were all round me and all yelling out together what should or should not be done, and what would happen if we did or did not do it. It was babel and bedlam let loose.

With the first plunge the crocodile disappeared, but it came up again ten metres away thrashing the water into foam and going upstream like a paddle-boat gone reeling roaring mad — if one can imagine such a thing. I had another shot at him the instant he reappeared, but one could neither see nor hear where it struck, and again and again I fired whenever he showed up for a second. He appeared to be shot through the lungs. At any rate the men on the other bank, who were then quite close enough to see, said that it was so. The wagon drive had run down the bank out on to the first sand spit and I followed them, shouting to the people opposite to get out of the line of fire, as I could no longer shoot without risk of hitting them.

The crocodile after his first straight dash upstream tacked about in all directions, disappearing for short spells and plunging out again in unexpected places. One of these sudden reappearances brought him once more abreast, and quite near to us. Jim with a fierce yell and his assegai held high in his right hand dashed into the water, going through the shallows in wild leaps. I called to him to come back but against his yells and the excited shouts of the ever-increasing crowd my voice could not live, and Jim, mad with excitement, went on. Twenty metres out, where increasing depth steadied him, he turned for a moment and seeing himself alone in the water called to me with eager confidence, 'Come on, Baas.'

It had never occurred to me that anyone would be such an idiot as to go into water after a wounded crocodile. There was no need to finish off this one, for it was bound to die, and no one wanted the meat or skin. Who, then, would be so mad as to think of such a thing? Five minutes earlier I would have answered very confidently for myself, but there are times when one cannot afford to be sensible. There was a world of unconscious irony in Jim's choice of words *'Come on!'* and *'Baas!'*

The servant giving the lead to his master was too much for me, and in I went.

I cannot say that there was much enjoyment in it for the first few moments — not until the excitement took hold and all else was forgotten. The first thing that struck me was that in the deep water my rifle was worth no more than a walking-stick, and not nearly as useful as an assegai. But what drove this and many other thoughts from my mind in a second was the appearance of Jock on the stage and his sudden jump into the leading place.

In the first confusion he had passed unnoticed, probably at my heels as usual, but the instant I answered Jim's challenge by jumping into the water he gave one whimpering yelp of excitement and plunged in too. In a few seconds he had outdistanced us all and was leading straight for the crocodile. I shouted to him but of course he heard nothing, and Jim and I plunged and struggled along to head the dog off.

As the crocodile came up Jock went straight for him. His eyes were gleaming, his shoulders were up, his nose was out, and his neck was stretched to the utmost in his eagerness as he ploughed along straining every muscle to catch up. When the crocodile went under he slackened and looked anxiously about, but each fresh rise was greeted

210

by whimpering yelps of intense suppressed excitement as he fairly hoisted himself out of the water with the vigour of his swimming.

The water was now breast-high for us, and we were far out in the stream when the men on the bank got their first chance and a flight of assegais went at the enemy as he rose. Several struck and two remained in him. He rose again a few metres from Jim, and that sportsman let fly one that struck well home. Jock, who had been toiling close behind for some time, and gaining slowly, was not five metres off then. The floundering and lashing of the crocodile were bewildering, but on he went as grimly and eagerly as ever. I fired again — not more than eight metres away — but the water was then up to my arms, and it was impossible to pick a vital part. The brain and neck were the only spots to finish him, but one could see nothing beyond a great upheaval of water, clouds of spray and blood-stained foam.

The crocodile turned from the shot and dived upstream, heading straight for Jock. The din of yelling voices stopped instantly as the huge open-mouthed thing plunged towards the dog, and for one sick horrified moment I stood and watched — helpless.

Had the crocodile risen in front of Jock that would have been the end — one snap would have done it. But it passed clear underneath, and, coming up just beyond him, the great lashing tail sent the dog up with a column of water almost a metre in the air. Jock did as he had done when the kudu bull tossed him. His head was round straining to get at the croco-

211

dile before he was able to turn his body in the water, and the silence was broken by a yell of wild delight and approval from the bank.

Before us the water was too deep and the stream too strong to stand in. Jim in his eagerness had gone in shoulder-high, and my rifle when aimed only just cleared the water. The crocodile was the mark for more assegais from the bank as it charged upstream again, with Jock tailing behind, and it was then easy enough to follow its movements by the shafts that were never all submerged. The struggles became perceptibly weaker, and as it turned again to go with the stream every effort was concentrated on killing and landing it before it reached the rocks and rapids.

I moved back for higher ground and, finding that the bed shelved up rapidly downstream, made for a position where there would be enough elevation to put in a brain shot. The water was not more than waist-high then, and as the crocodile came rolling and thrashing down I waited for his head to show up clearly. My right foot touched a sloping rock which rose almost to the surface of the water close above the rapids, and anxious to get the best possible position for a last shot, I took my stand there. The rock was the ordinary shelving bedrock, uptilted at an easy angle and cut off sheer on the exposed side, and the wave in the current would have shown this to any one not wholly occupied with other things. But I had eyes for nothing except the crocodile which was then less than a dozen metres off, and in my anxiety to secure a firm footing for the shot I moved the right foot again and it went over the edge of the rock. The result was as complete a spill as if one unthinkingly stepped backwards off a diving board. I disappeared in deep water, with the knowledge that the crocodile would join me there in a few seconds.

One never knows how these things are done or how long they take. I was back on the rock — without the rifle — and had the water out of my eyes in time to see the crocodile roll helplessly by, 2 metres away, with Jock behind making excited but ridiculously futile attempts to get hold of the tail. Jim — swimming, plunging and blowing like a maddened hippo — formed the tail of the procession, which was headed by my waterlogged hat floating heavily a metre or so in front of the crocodile.

While the crowd of yelling spectators under the generalship of Jim were landing the crocodile, I had time to do some diving, and managed to fish out my rifle.

My Sunday change was wasted. But we got the crocodile, and that was something, after all.

The Fighting Baboon

On the way to Lydenburg, not many treks from Paradise Camp, we outspanned for the day at a well-known and much-frequented public outspan. A fair-sized wayside store marked its importance. After breakfast we went to the store to swap news with the men on the spot and a couple of horsemen who had off-saddled there.

There were several other houses of sorts. They were rough wattle and daub erections which were called houses, as an acknowledgement of pretensions expressed in the rectangular shape and corrugated iron roof. One of these belonged to Seedling, the field cornet and only official in the district. He was the petty local justice who was supposed to administer minor laws, collect certain revenues and taxes, and issue passes. The salary was nominal, but the position bristled with opportunities for one who was not very particular; and the then occupant of the office seemed well enough pleased with the arrangement, whatever the public may have thought of it.

He was neither popular nor trusted. There were many tales of great harshness, injustice, corruption and favouritism in his dealings with White and Black men.

This, added to habitual drunkenness and uncertain temper, made a formidable tally in the account against him. He was also a bully and a coward, and all knew it; but unfortunately he was the law — as it stood for us.

Seedling, although an official of the Boer government, was an Englishman. There were several of them on the gold-fields in those days, and for the most part, they were

214

good fellows and good officials — this one was an exception. We all knew him personally. He was effusively friendly, and we suffered him and — paid for the drinks. That was in his public capacity. In his private capacity he was the owner of the fighting baboon of evil and cruel repute.

If ever fate's instruments moved unconscious of their mission and the part they were to play, it is certain that Jock and Jim Makokel' did so that day — the day that was the beginning of Seedling's fall and end.

It is not very clear how the trouble began. We had been sitting on the little store-counter and talking for over an hour, a group of half a dozen, swapping off the news of the gold-fields and the big world; against that from Delagoa Bay and the bushveld.

Seedling joined us early and, as usual, began the morning with drinks. We were not used to that on the road, or out hunting; indeed, we rarely took any drink. But we had one round of drinks which was 'called' by one of the horsemen, and then, to return the compliment, another round called by one of us. A few minutes later Seedling announced effusively that it was his 'shout'. But it was only ten in the morning, and those who had taken spirits had had enough. Thus Seedling's round was reduced to himself and the proprietor. No man however thirsty would drink alone in those days — it was taken as a mark of meanness or evidence of 'soaking' — and the proprietor had to be ready at any time to 'take one for the good of the house'.

A quarter of an hour passed, and Seedling, who had said nothing since his 'shout' was declined, turned away and strolled out, with hands thrust deep in the pockets of his riding breeches and a long heavy sjambok dangling from one wrist. There was silence as he moved through the doorway, and when the square patch of sunlight on the earth floor was again unbroken the man behind the counter remarked:

'Too long between drinks for him. Gone for a pull at the private bottle.'

'Is that how it's going?'

'Yah! his liquor's took him wrong today — you'll see!'

We did see. We had forgotten Seedling, and were hearing all about the new finds reported from Barberton district, when one of the wagon drivers came running into the store calling to me, 'Baas, Baas! come quickly! The baboon has got Jock. It will kill him!'

I had known all about the vicious brute, and had often heard of Seedling's fiendish delight in arranging fights, or enticing dogs to attack it for the pleasure of seeing the beast kill the outmatched dogs. The dog had no chance at all, for the baboon remained out of reach in his house on the pole as long as it chose, and made its rush when it would tell best. But apart from this the baboon was an exceptionally big and powerful one, and it is very doubtful if any dog could have tackled it successfully in an open fight. The creature was clever. Its enormous jaws and teeth were quite equal to the biggest dog's and it had the advantage of four 'hands'.

Its tactics in a fight were quite simple and most effective. With its front feet it caught the dog by the ears or neck, holding the head so that there was no risk of being bitten, and then gripping the body lower down with the hind feet, it tore lumps out of the throat, breast and stomach — pushing with all four feet and tearing with the terrible teeth. The poor dogs were hopelessly outmatched.

I did not see the beginning of Jock's encounter, but the drivers' stories pieced together told everything. It appears

216

that when Seedling left the store he went into his own hut and remained there some little time. On coming out again he strolled over to the baboon's pole about half-way between the two houses and began teasing it, throwing pebbles at it to see it dodge and duck behind the pole, and then flicking at it with the sjambok, amused by its frightened and angry protests. While he was doing this, Jock, who had followed me to the store, strolled out again making his way towards the wagons.

The baboon had taken refuge in its box on top of the pole to escape the sjambok, and when Seedling saw Jock come out he commenced whistling and calling softly to him. Jock, of course, heard nothing; but he may have responded mildly to the friendly overtures conveyed by the extended hand and patting of legs, or more probably simply took the nearest way to the wagon where he might sleep in peace. What the drivers agree on is that as Jock passed the pole Seedling patted and held him; at the same time he called the baboon and gave Jock a push which upset his balance. Jock naturally jumped round and faced Seedling, which meant he had his back to the baboon. He could not hear the rattle of the chain on the box and pole and saw nothing of the charging brute. It was the purest accident that the dog stood centimetres out of reach. The baboon — chained by the neck instead of the waist, because it used to bite through all loin straps — made its rush, but the chain brought it up before its hands could reach Jock and threw the hindquarters round with such force

against him that Jock was sent rolling metres away. I can well believe that this second attack from a different and wholly unexpected quarter thoroughly roused him, and can picture how he turned to face it.

It was at this moment that Jim first noticed what was going on. It was the hoarse threatening shout of the baboon as it jumped at Jock, as much as the exclamations of the men that roused Jim. He knew instantly what was on, and grabbing a stick made a dash to save the dog, with the others following him.

While Jock was spinning in the dust the baboon recovered itself, and standing up on its hind legs, reached out its long ungainly arms towards him, and let out a shout of defiance. Jock regaining his feet dashed in, jumped aside and feinted again and again, as he had learnt to do when big horns swished at him. He kept out of reach just as he had done ever since the duiker taught him the use of its hoofs. He knew what to do, just as he had known how to swing the porcupine. For all the fighting fury that possessed him, the dog took the measure of the chain and kept outside it. Round and round he flew, darting in, jumping back, snapping and dodging, but never getting right home.

The baboon was as clever as he was. At times it jumped about a metre in the air, straight up, in the hope that Jock would run underneath. At others, it would make a sudden lunge with the long arms, or a more surprising reach out with the hind legs to grab him. Then the baboon began gradually to reduce its circle, leaving behind enough slack chain for a spring; but Jock was not to be drawn. In cleverness they were well matched — neither made or lost a point.

When Jim rushed up to save Jock, his eager anxious shouts of the dog's name warned Seedling and made him turn. As Jim ran forward the White man stepped out to stop him.

'Leave the dog alone!' he shouted, pale with anger.

'Baas, Baas, the dog will be killed', Jim called excitedly, as he tried to get round. The White man made a jump towards him, and with a backhand slash of the sjambok struck him across the face, shouting at him again: 'Leave him, I tell you.'

Jim jumped back, thrusting out his stick to guard against

another vicious cut, and so it went on with alternate slash and guard, and the big Zulu danced round with nimble bounds, guarding, dodging, or bearing the sjambok cuts, to save the dog. Seedling was mad with rage, for who had ever heard of a Black man standing up to a field cornet? Still Jim would not give way. He kept trying to get in front of Jock, to head him off the fight, and all the while shouting to the other drivers to call me. But Seedling was the field cornet, and not one of them dared to move against him.

At last the baboon, finding that Jock would not come on, tried other tactics. It made a sudden retreat and, rushing for the pole, hid behind it as for protection. Jock made a jump and the baboon leaped out to meet him, but the dog stopped at the chain's limit, and the baboon, just as in the first dash, overshot the mark. It was brought up by the jerk of the collar, and for one second sprawled on its back. That was the first chance for Jock and he took it. With one spring he was in. His head shot between the baboon's hind legs, and with his teeth buried in the soft stomach he lay back and pulled — pulled for dear life, as he had pulled and dragged on the legs of wounded game; tugged as he had tugged at the porcupine; held on as he had held when the kudu bull wrenched and strained every bone and muscle in his body.

Then came the sudden turn. As Jock fastened on to the baboon, dragging taut the chain while the screaming brute struggled on its back, Seedling stood for a second irresolute, and then with a stride forward raised his sjambok to strike the dog. That was too much for Jim. He made a spring in and grasping the raised sjambok with his left hand held Seedling powerless, while in his right he raised his stick on guard.

'Let him fight, Baas. You said it. Let the dog fight!' he panted, hoarse with excitement.

The White man, livid with fury, struggled and kicked, but the wrist loop of his sjambok held him prisoner and he could do nothing.

That was the moment when a panic-stricken driver plucked up courage enough to call me, and that was the scene we saw as we ran out of the little shop. Jim would not strike the White man, but his face was a muddy grey, and it was written there that he would rather die than give up the dog.

Before I reached them it was clear to us all what had happened. Jim was protesting to Seedling and at the same time calling to me. It was a jumble, but a jumble eloquent enough for us, and all intelligible. Jim's excited gabble was addressed with reckless incoherence to Seedling, to me, and to Jock.

'You threw him in. You tried to kill him. He did it. It was not the dog. Kill him, Jock, kill him. Leave him, let him fight. You said it — let him fight. Kill him, Jock. Kill! Kill! Kill!'

Then Seedling did the worst thing possible; he turned on me with:

'Call off your dog, I tell you, or I'll shoot him and your ——— driver too!'

'We'll see about that! They can fight it out now', I said. I took the sjambok from Jim's hand, and cut it from the White man's wrist.

'Now. Stand back.'

And he stood back.

The baboon was quite helpless. Powerful as the brute was, and formidable as were the arms and gripping feet, it had no chance while Jock could keep his feet and had strength to drag and hold the chain tight. The collar was choking it, and the grip on the stomach — the baboon's own favourite and most successful device — was fatal.

220

It was not justice to call Jock off, but I did it. The cruel brute deserved killing, but the human look and cries and behaviour of the baboon were too sickening; and Seedling went into his hut without even a look at his stricken champion.

Jock stood off, with his mouth open from ear to ear. His red tongue was dangling, he was bloodstained and panting, but his eager feet were ever on the move shifting from spot to spot, his ears going back and forward, and his eyes — now on the baboon and now on me — pleading for the sign to go in again.

Before evening the baboon was dead.

The day's excitement was too much for Jim. After singing and dancing himself into a frenzy round Jock, after shouting the whole story of the fight in violent and incessant gabble over and over again to those who had witnessed it, after making every ear ring and every head swim with his mad din, he grabbed his sticks once more and made off for one of the kraals, there to find drink for which he thirsted body and soul.

In the afternoon the sudden scattering of the inhabitants of a small kraal on the hillside opposite, and some lusty shouting, drew attention that way. Jim had found his drink.

We were loaded for Lydenburg — another week's trekking through and over the mountains — and as we intended coming back the same way a fortnight later I decided at once to leave Jim at his kraal, which was only a little further on, and pick him up on the return journey.

I nearly always paid him off in livestock or sheep. He had good wages, and for many months at a time would draw no money. He was a splendid worker and as true as steel, so that, in spite of all the awful worry I had a soft spot for Jim and had taken a good deal of trouble on his account. He got his pay at the end of the trip or the season, but not in cash. It was invested for him — greatly to his disgust at the time I am bound to say — in livestock, so that he would not be able to squander it in drink or be robbed of it while incapable.

Jim's gloomy dignity was colossal when it came to squaring

up and I invited him to state what he wished me to buy for him. To be treated like an irresponsible child, to be chaffed and cheerfully warned by me, to be met by the giggles and squirts of laughter of the others, for whom he had the most profound contempt, and worst of all to see the respectable Sam counting out with awkward eager hands and gleaming eyes the good red gold, while he, Makokela the Zulu, was treated like a piccanin — ugh. It was horrible. Intolerable!

Jim would hold aloof in injured gloomy silence, not once looking at me, but standing sideways and staring stonily past me into the far distance, and not relaxing for a second the expression of profound displeasure on his weather-beaten face. No joke or chaff, no question or reason, would move him to even look my way. All he would do was, now and again, give a click of disgust, a quick shake of the head, and say, 'Aug! Ang-a-funa!' (I do not desire it!)

We had the same fight over and over again, but I always won in the end. When it was all over Jim recovered rapidly. At parting time there was the broadest of grins and a stentorian shout of 'Hlala Kahle! Inkos!' Jim went off with his springy walk, swinging his sticks and jabbering his thoughts aloud, evidently about me, for every now and again he would spring lightly into the air, twirl the stick, and shout a deep-throated 'Inkos!' full of the joy of living.

This time Jim was too fully wound up to be dealt with as before, and I simply turned him off, telling him to come to the camp in a fortnight's time.

I was a day behind the wagons when we returned, and riding up to the camp towards midday I found Jim waiting for me. He looked ill and shrunken, wrapped in an old coat and squatting against the wall of the little hut. As I passed he rose slowly and gave his 'Sakubona! Inkos!' with that curious controlled air by which he managed to suggest a kind of fatalist resignation or indifference touched with disgust. There was something wrong, so I rode past without stopping — one learns to find out how the land lies before doing anything.

It was a bad story, almost as bad as one would think possible where civilised beings are concerned. Jim's own story lacked certain details of which he was necessarily ignorant; it also omitted the fact that he had been drunk, but in the main it was quite true.

This is what happened. Several days after our departure Jim went down to the store again and raised some liquor. He was not fighting, but he was noisy, and was the centre of a small knot of shouting, arguing men near the store when Seedling returned after a two days' absence.

No doubt it was unfortunate that the very first thing Seedling saw on his return was the man who had defied him and who was the cause of his humiliation. That that man should by his behaviour give the slenderest excuse for interference was in the last degree unlucky.

Seedling's mind was made up from the moment he set eyes on Jim. Throwing the reins over his horse's head he walked into the excited gabbling knot, and laid about him with the sjambok, scattering and silencing them instantly. He then took Jim by the wrist saying, 'I want you.' He called to someone to bring a reim, and leading Jim over to the side of the store tied him up to the horse rail with arms at full stretch. Taking out his knife he cut Jim's clothing down the back so that it fell away in two halves in front of him. Then he took off his own coat and flogged him with his sjambok.

I would like to tell all that happened because it would explain the murderous man-hunting feeling that possessed us when we heard it. But it was too cruel. Let it be. Only one thing to show the spirit: twice during the flogging Seedling stopped to go into the store for a drink.

Jim crawled home to find his kraal ransacked and deserted, and his wives and children driven off in panic. In addition to the flogging Seedling had, in accordance with his practice, imposed fines far beyond Jim's means in cash, so as to provide an excuse for seizing what he wanted. The police had raided the kraal, and the cattle and goats — his only property — were gone.

He told it all in a dull monotone. For the time the life and fire were gone out of him; but he was not cowed, not broken. There was a curl of contempt on his mouth and in his tone that whipped the white skin on my own back and made it all a disgrace unbearable. That this should be the reward for his courageous defence of Jock seemed too awful.

We went inside to talk it over and make our plans. The wagons should go on next day as if nothing had happened, Jim remaining in one of the half-tents or elsewhere out of sight of passers-by. I was to ride into Lydenburg and lodge information — for in such a case the authorities would surely act. That was the best, or at any rate the first, course to be tried.

There was no difficulty about the warrant, for there were many counts in the indictment against Seedling. But even so worthless a brute as that seemed to have one friend, or perhaps an accomplice, to give him warning, and before we reached his quarters with the police he had cleared on horseback for Portuguese territory, taking with him a lead horse.

We got most of Jim's cattle back for him — which he seemed to consider the main thing — but we were sorely disgusted at the man's escape.

That was the year of the gold-rush. Thousands of newcomers poured into the country on the strength of the gold discoveries. Materials and provisions of all kinds were almost unprocurable and stood at famine prices, and consequently we — the transport riders — reaped a golden harvest. Never had there been such times. Wagons and spans were paid for in single trips, and so great was the demand for supplies that some refused transport and bought their own goods, which they resold on the gold-fields at prices twice as profitable as the highest rates of transport.

Thus the days lost in the attempt to catch Seedling were valuable days. The season was limited, and as early rains might cut us off, a few days thrown away might mean the loss of a whole trip.

Near the Crocodile on our way down to Delagoa Bay we heard from men coming up that Seedling had been there some days before but that, hearing we were on the way down and had sworn to shoot him, he had ridden on to Komati, leaving one horse behind bad with horse sickness. The report about shooting him was, of course, ridiculous — probably his own imagination — but it was some comfort to know that he was in such a state of terror that his own fancies were hunting him down.

At Komati we learned that he had stayed three days at the store of that Goanese murderer, Antonio. Antonio, suspecting something wrong about a White man who came on horseback and dawdled aimlessly three days at Komati Drift, going indoors whenever a stranger appeared, wormed the secret out with liquor and sympathy. When he had got most of Seedling's money out of him, by pretence of bribing the Portuguese officials and getting news, he made a bold bid for the rest by saying that a warrant was out for him in

Delagoa and he must on no account go on. He no doubt hoped to get the horse, saddle and bridle, as well as the cash, and was quite prepared to drug Seedling when the time came, and slip him quietly into the Komati at night where the crocodiles would take care of the evidence.

Antonio, however, overshot the mark. Seedling, who knew all about him, took fright, saddled up and bolted up the river meaning to make for the Lebombo, near the Tembe Drift, where Bob McNab and his merry comrades ran free of governments and were a law unto themselves. It was no place for a nervous man, but Seedling had no choice, and he went on. He had liquor in his saddle-bags and food for several days. But he was not used to the bush.

Those from whom he asked directions said that he bought beer from them, but did not want food; for he looked sick. He was red and swollen in the face, and his eyes were wild. The horse was weak and also looked sick, being very thin and empty, but they showed him the footpath over the hills which would take him to Tom's — a White man's store on the road to Delagoa — and he left them. That was Tom Barnett's at Piscene, where we always stopped, for Tom was a good friend of ours.

That was how we came to meet Seedling again. He had made a loop of at least 250 kilometres in four days in his efforts to avoid us, but he was waiting for us when we arrived at Tom Barnett's. We who had hurried on to catch him, believing that the vengeance of justice depended on us, forgot that it had been otherwise decreed.

Tom stood in the doorway of his store as we walked up — 1,5 metres in his boots, but every centimetre of it a man — with his hands resting idly on his hips and a queer smile on his face as he nodded welcome.

'Did a White man come here on horseback during the last few days from the drift?'

'No!'

'On foot?'

'No, not the whole way.'

'Is he here now?'

Tom nodded.

'You know about him, Tom?'

'Seedling. The chap you're after, isn't it?'

'Yes', we answered, lowering our voices.

Tom looked from one to the other with the same queer smile, and then making a move to let us into the store said quietly, 'He won't clear, boys. He's dead!'

Some men coming along the footpath had found the horse dead of horse sickness half a day away, and further on — a kilometre or so from the store — the rider lying on his back in the sun, dying of thirst. He died before they got him in.

Jim sat by himself the whole evening and never spoke a word.

The Last Trek

It was Pettigrew's Road that brought home to me, and to others, the wisdom of the old transport-riders' maxim: 'Take no risks'. We all knew that there were 'fly' belts on the old main road but we rushed these at night, for we knew enough of the tsetse fly to avoid it. However, the discovery of the new road to Barberton, a short cut with plenty of water and grass, which offered the chance of working an extra trip into the short Delagoa season, tempted me, among others, to take a risk.

We had seen no 'fly' when riding through to spy out the land, and again on the trip down with empty wagons all had seemed to be well; but I had good reason afterwards to recall that hurried trip down and the night spent at Louw's Creek. It was a lovely moonlight night, cool and still, and the grass was splendid. After many weeks of poor feeding and drought the cattle revelled in the land of plenty. We had timed our treks so as to get through the suspected parts of the road at night, believing that the fly did not trouble after dark.

Thus we were that night outspanned in the worst spot of all. I moved among the cattle myself, watching them feed greedily and waiting to see them satisfied before in-spanning again to trek through the night to some higher and more open ground. I noticed then that their tails were rather busy. At first it seemed the usual accompaniment of a good feed, an expression of satisfaction. After a while, however, the swishing became too vigorous for this, and when heads began to swing round and legs also were made use of, it seemed clear that something was worrying them. The older hands were so positive that at night cattle were safe from fly that it did not even then occur to me to suspect anything seriously wrong. Weeks passed by, and although the cattle became poorer, it was reasonable enough to put it down to the exceptional drought.

It was late in the season when we loaded up for the last time in Delagoa and ploughed our way through the Matolla swamp and the heavy sands at Piscene. Late as it was, there was no sign of rain, and the rain that we usually wanted to avoid would have been very welcome then. The roads were all blistering stones of powdery dust, and it was cruel work for man and beast.

The heat was intense, and there was no breeze. The dust moved along slowly apace with us in a dense cloud — men, wagons, and animals, all toned to the same hue; and the poor oxen toiling slowly along drew in the finely powdered stuff at every breath. At the outspan they stood about exhausted and panting, with rings and lines of brown marking where the moisture from nostrils, eyes and mouths had caught the dust and turned it into mud. At Matolla Poort, where the Lebombo Range runs low, the polished black rocks shone like anvils. The stones and baked earth scorched the feet of man and beast to aching and the world was like an oven. The heat came from above, below, around — a thousand glistening surfaces flashing back with intensity the sun's fierce rays. And there, at Matolla Poort, the big pool had given out.

Our stand-by was gone. There, in the deep cleft in the rocks where the feeding spring, cool and constant, had trickled down a smooth black rock beneath another over-hanging slab, and where ferns and mosses had clustered in one little spot in all the miles of blistering rocks, there

was nothing left but mud and slime. The water was as green and thick as pea soup; half a dozen rotting carcasses stuck in the mud round the one small wet spot where the pool had been — just where they fell and died. The coat had dropped away from some, and mats of hair, black brown and white, helped to thicken the green water. But we drank it. Sinking a handkerchief where the water looked thinnest and making a little well into which the moisture slowly filtered, we drank it greedily.

The next water on the road was Komati River, but the cattle were too weak to reach it in one trek, and remembering another pool off the road — a small lagoon found by accident when out hunting the year before — we moved on that night out on to the flats and made through the bush for several kilometres to look for water and grass.

We found the place just after dawn. There was a string of half a dozen pools ringed with yellow-plumed reeds — like a bracelet of sapphires set in gold — deep deep pools of beautiful water in the midst of a grand expanse of rich buffalo grass. It was too incredibly good.

I was trekking alone that trip, the only White man there, and — tired out by the all-night's work, the long ride, and the searching in the bush for the lagoon — I had gone to sleep after seeing the cattle to the water and grass. Before midday I was back among them again. Some odd movements struck a chord of memory and the night at Louw's Creek flashed back. Tails were swishing freely, and the bullock nearest me kicked up sharply at its side and swung its head round to brush something away.

I moved closer up to see what was causing the trouble. In a few minutes I heard a thin sing of wings, different from a mosquito's, and there settled on my shirt a grey fly, very like and not much larger than a common house-fly, whose wings folded over like a pair of scissors. That was the 'mark of the beast'. I knew then why this oasis had been left by transport-rider and trekker, as nature made it, untrodden and untouched.

Not a moment was lost in getting away from the 'fly'. But the mischief was already done. The cattle must have been bitten at Louw's Creek weeks before, and again that morning during the time I slept; and it was clear that, not drought and poverty, but fly was the cause of their weakness. After the first rains they would begin to die, and the right thing to do now was to press on as fast as possible and deliver the loads.

Barberton was booming and short of supplies, and the rates were the highest ever paid, but I had done better still, having bought my own goods, and the certain profit looked a fortune to me. Even if all the cattle became unfit for use or died, the loads would pay for everything and the right course therefore was to press on; for delay would mean losing both cattle and loads — all I had in the world — and starting again penniless with the years of hard work thrown away.

So the last hard struggle began. And it was work and puzzle day and night, without peace or rest. Trying to nurse the cattle in their daily failing strength, and yet to push them for all they could do; watching the sky cloud over every afternoon, promising rain that never came, and not knowing whether to call it promise or threat. For although rain would bring grass and water to save the cattle, it also meant death to the fly-bitten.

We crossed the Komati with three spans — forty-four oxen — to a wagon, for the drift was deep in two places and the weakened cattle could not keep their feet. It was a hard day, and by nightfall it was easy to pick out the oxen who would not last out a week. That night Zole lay down and did not get up again — Zole, the little fat schoolboy, always out of breath, always good-tempered and quiet, as tame as a pet dog.

He was the first to go. Day by day others followed. Some were only cattle, others were old friends and comrades on many a trek. The two big after-oxen Achmed and Bakir went down early. The Komati Drift had overtired them, and the weight and jolting of the heavy disselboom on the bad roads finished them off. These were the two inseparables who worked and grazed, walked and slept, side by side — never more than a few metres apart day or night since the day they became yokefellows. They died on consecutive days.

But the living wonder of that last trek was still old Zwaart-land the front ox. With his steady sober air, perfect under-

231

standing of his work, and firm clean buck-like tread, he still led the front span. Before we reached the Crocodile his mate gave in — worn to death by the ebbing of his own strength and by the steady indomitable courage of his comrade. Old Zwaartland pulled on, but my heart sank as I looked at him and noted the slightly 'staring' coat, the falling flanks, the tread less sure and brisk, and a look in his eyes that made me think he knew what was coming but would do his best.

The gallant-hearted old fellow held on. One after another we tried with him in the lead, half a dozen or more, but he wore them all down. In the dongas and spruits, where the crossings were often very bad and steep, the wagons would stick for hours, and the wear and strain on the exhausted cattle was killing: it was bad enough for the man who drove them. To see old Zwaartland then holding his ground, never for one moment turning or wavering while the others backed, jibbed and swayed and dragged him staggering backwards, made one's heart ache.

The worst of it was that with all the work and strain we accomplished less than we used to do before in a quarter of the time. Distances formerly covered in one trek took three, four, and even five now. Water, never too plentiful in certain parts, was sadly diminished by the drought, and it sometimes took us three or even four treks to get from water to water. Thus we had at times to drive the oxen back to the last place or on to the next one for their drinks, and by the time the poor beasts got back to the wagons to begin their trek they had done nearly as much as they were able to do.

And trouble begot trouble, as usual. Sam the respectable, who had drawn all his pay in Delagoa, gave up after one hard day and deserted me. He said that the hand of the Lord had smitten me and mine, and great misfortune would come to all. So, he left in the dark at Crocodile Drift, taking one of the leaders with him, and joined some wagons making for Lydenburg. The work was too hard for him. It was late in the season and he feared the rains and fever. He had no pluck or loyalty, and cared for no one but himself.

I was left with three leaders and two drivers to manage four wagons. It was Jim who told me of Sam's desertion. He had the cross, defiant, preoccupied look of old. But there was also something of satisfaction in his air as he walked up to me and stood to deliver the great vindication of his own unerring judgement.

'Sam has deserted you and taken his voorloper.' He jerked the words out at me, speaking in Zulu.

I said nothing. It was just about Sam's form. It annoyed but did not surprise me. Jim favoured me with a hard searching look, a subdued grunt, and a click expressive of things he could not put into words. He turned and walked back towards his wagon; but half-way to it he broke silence. Facing me once more, he thumped his chest and hurled at me in mixed Zulu and English, 'I said so. Sam lead a Bible. Sam no good. Umph! M'Shangaan. I said so. I always said so.'

When Jim helped me to inspan Sam's wagon, he did it to an accompaniment of Zulu imprecations which only a Zulu could properly appreciate. They were quite above my head, but every now and then I caught one sentence repeated like the responses in a litany: 'I'll kill that Shangaan when I see him again!'

At Lion Spruit there was more bad luck. Lions had been troublesome there in former years, but for a couple of seasons nothing had been seen of them. Their return was probably due to the fact that, because of the drought and consequent failure of other waters, the game on which they preyed had moved down towards the river. At any rate, they returned unexpectedly and we had one bad night when the cattle were unmanageable, and their nerves all on edge. The herdsmen had seen spoor in the afternoon. At dusk we heard the distant roaring, and later on, the nearer and more ominous grunting.

I fastened Jock up in the tent wagon lest the sight of him should prove too tempting. He was bristling like a hedgehog and constantly working out beyond the cattle, glaring and growling incessantly towards the bush. We had four big fires at the four corners of the outspan, and no doubt this saved a bad stampede, for in the morning we found a circle of spoor where the lions had walked round and round the outspan. There were scores of footprints — the tracks of at least four or five animals.

In the bushveld the oxen were invariably tied up at night, picketed to the trek-chain, each pair at its yoke ready to be inspanned for the early morning trek. Ordinarily the weight of the chain and yokes was sufficient to keep them in place, but when there were lions about, and the cattle liable to be scared and all to sway off together in the same direction, we took the extra precaution of pegging down the chain and anchoring the front yoke to a tree or stake.

We had a lot of trouble that night, as one of the lions persistently took his stand to windward of the cattle to scare them with his scent. We knew well enough when he was there, although unable to see anything, as all the oxen would face upwind, staring with bulging eyeballs in that direction and braced up tense with excitement. If one of them made a sudden move, the whole lot jumped in response and swayed off downwind away from the danger, dragging the gear with them and straining until the heavy wagons yielded to the tug. We had to run out and drive them up again to stay the stampede. It is a favourite device of lions, when tackling camps and outspans, for one of them to go to windward so that the terrified animals on winding him may stampede in the opposite direction where the other lions are lying in wait.

Two oxen broke away that night and were never seen again. Once I saw a low light-coloured form steal across the road, and took a shot at it, but rifle shooting at night is a gamble, and there was no sign of a hit.

I was too short-handed and too pressed for time to make a real try for the lions next day, and after a morning spent in fruitless search for the lost bullocks we went on again.

Instead of twenty to thirty kilometres a day, as we should

have done, we were then making between six and twelve — and sometimes not one. The heat and the drought were awful. At last we reached the Crocodile and struck up the right bank for the short cut — Pettigrew's Road — to Barberton, and there we had good water and some pickings of grass and young reeds along the river bank.

Then, as we crawled slowly along the river bank, came one black day which is not to be forgotten. In one of the cross-spruits cutting sharply down to the river the second wagon stuck. The poor tired-out cattle were too weak and dispirited to pull it out. Being short of drivers and leaders it was necessary to do the work in turns, that is, after getting one wagon through a bad place, to go back for another. We had to double-span this wagon, taking the span from the front wagon back to hook on in front of the other and on this occasion I led the span while Jim drove.

We were all tired out by the work and heat, and I lay down in the dusty road in front of the oxen to rest while the chains were being coupled up. I looked up into old Zwaartland's eyes, deep, placid, constant, dark grey eyes — the ox-eyes of which so many speak and write and so few really know. There was trouble in them. He looked anxious and hunted, and it made me heartsick to see it.

When the pull came, the back span, already disheartened and out of hand, swayed and turned every way, straining the front oxen to the utmost; yet Zwaartland took the strain and pulled. For a few moments both front oxen stood firm and then his mate cut it and turned. The team swung away with a rush, and the old fellow was jerked backwards and rolled over on his side. He struggled gamely, but it was some minutes before he could rise; and then his eye looked wilder and more despairing, his legs were planted apart to balance him, and his flanks were quivering.

Jim straightened up the double span again. Zwaartland leaned forward once more, and the others followed his lead. The wagon moved a little and they managed to pull it out. But I, walking in front, felt the brave old fellow stagger, and saw him, with head lowered, plod blindly like one stricken to death.

We outspanned on the rise, and I told Jim to leave the reim on Zwaartland's head. Many a good turn from him deserved one more from me — the last. I sent Jim for the rifle, and led the old front ox to the edge of the donga where a bleached tree lay across it. . . He dropped into the donga under the dead tree, and I packed the dry branches over him and set fire to the pile. It looks absurd now, but to leave him to the wolf and the jackal seemed like going back on a friend. The queer looks of the wagon drivers were easier to bear. Jim watched, but said nothing. With a single grunt and a shrug of his shoulders he stalked back to the wagons.

The talk that night at the drivers' fire went on in low-pitched tones — not a single word audible to me, but I knew what it was about. As Jim stood up to get his blanket off the waggon, he stretched himself and closed off the evening's talk with his Zulu click and the remark that 'All White men are mad, in some way.'

So we crawled on until we reached the turn where the road turned between the mountain range and the river and where the railway runs today. There, we outspanned one day when the heat became so great that it was no longer possible to go on. For weeks the storm-clouds had gathered, threatened, and dispersed. Thunder had come half-heartedly, little spots of rain enough to pock-mark the dust; but there had been no break in the drought.

It was past noon that day when everything grew still. The birds and insects hushed their sound and the dry leaves did not give a whisper. There was the warning in the air that one knows but cannot explain; and it struck me and the drivers together that it was time to spread and tie down the

236

buck-sails which we had not unfolded for months.

While we were busy at this there came an unheralded flash and crash. A few big drops fell; and then the flood-gates were opened and the reservoir of the long months of drought was turned loose on us.

Little enough could one realise in those first few minutes, yet there are details, unnoticed at the time, which come back quite vividly when the bewildering rush is over, and there are impressions which it is not possible to forget.

There were sounds and smells and sights. The sounds that began with the sudden crash of thunder and the dead silence that followed it. The first great drops that fell with such pats on the dust, then more and faster — yet still so big and separate as to make one look round to see where they fell. The sound on the wagon-sail — at first as of bouncing marbles, then the 'devil's tattoo', and then the roar!

And outside there was the muffled puff and patter in the dust; the rustle as the drops struck dead leaves and grass and sticks; the blend of many notes that made one great sound, always growing, changing and moving on — full of weird significance — until there came the steady swish and hiss of water upon water, when the earth had ceased to stand up against the rain and was swamped. But even that did not last, for then the fallen rain raised its voice against the rest, and little sounds of trickling scurrying waters came to tone the ceaseless hiss, and grew and grew until from every side the chorus of rushing tumbling waters filled the air with the steady roar of the flood.

And the smells! The smell of the baked drought-bound earth; the faint clearing and purifying by the first few drops; the mingled dust and damp; the rinsed air; the clean sense of water, water everywhere; and in the end the bracing sensation in nostrils and head of, not wind exactly, but of swirling air thrust out to make room for the falling rain; and, when all was over, the sense of glorious clarified air and scoured earth — the smell of a new-washed world!

And the things that one saw went with the rest, marking the stages of the storm's short vivid life. The first puffs of dust, where drops struck like bullets, and cloud that rose to meet them. The drops themselves that streaked slanting down like a flight of steel ramrods. I had seen the yellow-brown ground change colour. In a few seconds it was damp, then mud, then all asheen. A minute more, and busy little trickles started everywhere — tiny things centimetres long, and while one watched them they joined and merged, hurrying on with twist and turn, but ever onward to a given point — to meet like the veins in a leaf. Each tuft of grass became a fountain-head. Each space between, a little rivulet, racing away with its burden of leaf and twig and dust and foam until in a few minutes all were lost in one sheet of moving water.

Crouching under the wagon I watched it and saw the little streamlets, dirty and debris-laden, steal slowly on like sluggard snakes down to my feet and, winding round me, meet beyond and hasten on. Soon the grass tufts and higher spots were wet, and as the water rose on my boots and the splash beat up to my knees, it seemed worth while making for the tent of the wagon. But in there the roar was deafening. The rain beat down with such force that it drove through the canvas-covered wagon-tent and greased buck-sail in fine mist. In there it was black dark, and tarpaulin covering all, and I slipped out again back to my place under the wagon to watch the storm.

When the rain ceased the air was full of the roar of waters, growing louder and nearer all the time. I walked down the long low spur to look at the river, expecting much, and was grievously disappointed. It was no fuller and not much changed.

How small the great storm seemed then.

There are few things more deceptive than the tropical storm. To one caught in it, all the world seems deluged and overwhelmed, yet not far away it may be all peace and sunshine. I looked at the river and laughed — at myself. The revelation seemed complete. One felt so small. Still, the drought was broken, the rains had come, and in spite of disappointment I stayed to watch, drawn by the scores of little things caught up and carried by — the first harvest garnered by the rains.

A quarter of an hour or more may have been spent thus, when amid all the chorus of the rushing waters there stole in a duller murmur. Murmur it was at first, but it grew steadily

238

into a low-toned, monotoned, distant roar, and it caught and held one like the roar of coming hail or hurricane. It was the river coming down.

The sun was out again, and in the straight reach above the bend there was every chance to watch the flood from the bank where I stood. It seemed strangely long in coming, but come it did at last, in waves like the half-spent breakers on a sandy beach. Heavens what a scene! The racing waves, each dashing for the foremost place; the tall reeds caught waist high and then laid low, their silvery tops dipped, hidden and drowned in the flood; the trees yielding, and the branches snapping like matches and twirling like feathers down the stream; the rumbling thunder of big boulders loosed and tumbled, rolled like marbles on the rocks below; whole trees brought down, and turning helplessly in the flood. It was tremendous; and one had to stay and watch.

Then the waves ceased, and behind the opposite bank another stream began to make its way, winding like a huge snake, spreading wider as it went across the flats beyond, until the two rejoined and the river became one again. The roar of waters gradually lessened, and looking down I saw the fall was gone and that water ran to water — swift as ever, but voiceless now — and was lost in the river itself. By centimetres the water rose towards my feet. The yellow scum-flecked water worked silently up the dongas, reaching out with stealthy feelers to enclose the place where I was standing; and then it was time to go.

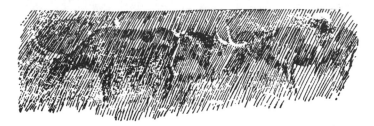

The cattle had turned their tails to the storm, and stood it out. They too were washed clean and looked fresher and brighter, but there was nothing in that. Two of them had been seen moving slowly down the slope from the out-

239

span, stung by the heavy drops and yielding in their weakness to the easy gradient. Only fifty metres away they should have stopped in the hollow — the shallow dry donga of the morning; but they were gone. Unwilling to turn back and face the rain, they had no doubt been caught in the rush of storm-water and swirled away, and their bodies were bobbing in the Crocodile many kilometres below by the time we missed them.

In a couple of hours the water had run off. The flooded dongas were almost dry again, and we moved on.

It was then that the real 'rot' set in. Next morning there were half a dozen oxen unable to stand up, and again the following day. It was no longer possible to take the four wagons; all the spare cattle had been used up and it was better to face the worst at once. So, I distributed the best of the load on the other three wagons and abandoned the rest of it with the fourth wagon in the bush. But day by day the oxen dropped out, until eventually there were not enough left for the three wagons.

This time it meant abandoning both wagon and load. I gave the cattle a day's rest then, hoping that they would pick up strength on good grass to face the eight drifts that lay between us and Barberton.

Our Last Hunt

We had not touched fresh meat for many days, as there had been no time for shooting; but I knew that game was plentiful across the river in the rough country between the Kaap and Crocodile, and I started off to make the best of the day's delay, little dreaming that it was to be the last time Jock and I would hunt together.

Weeks had passed without a hunt, and Jock must have thought there was a sad falling away on the part of his master. He no longer expected anything. The rifle was never taken down now except for an odd shot from the outspan or to put some poor animal out of its misery. Since the night with the lions, when he had been ignominiously cooped up, there had been nothing to stir his blood and make life worth living.

This morning as he saw me rise from breakfast and proceed to potter about the wagons in the way he had come to regard as inevitable, he looked on indifferently for a few minutes and then stretched out full length in the sun and went to sleep.

241

I could not take him with me across the river, as the fly was said to be bad there, and it was no place to risk horse or dog. The best of prospects would not have tempted me to take a chance with him, but I hated ordering him to stay behind, as it hurt his dignity and sense of comradeship, so it seemed a happy accident that he was asleep and I could slip away unseen. As the cattle were grazing along the river bank only a few hundred metres off, I took a turn that way to have a look at them, with natural but quite fruitless concern for their welfare, and a moment later met the herdsman running towards me and calling out excitedly something which I made out to be:

'Crocodile! Crocodile, Inkos! A crocodile has taken one of the oxen.' The waggon drivers heard it also, and armed with assegais and sticks were on the bank almost as soon as I was. but there was no sign of crocodile or bullock. The man showed us the place where the weakened animal had gone down to drink — the hoof slides were plain enough — and told how, as it drank, the long black coffin-head had appeared out of the water.

He described stolidly how the big jaws had opened and gripped the bullock's nose. How he, a few metres away, had seen the struggle and how he had shouted and hurled his sticks and stones and tufts of grass, and feinted to rush down at it; and how, after a muffled bellow, and a weak staggering effort to pull back, the poor beast had slid out into the deep water and disappeared. It seemed to be a quite unnecessary addition to my troubles. Misfortunes were coming thick and fast.

Half and hour was wasted in watching and searching, but we saw no more of crocodile or bullock, and as there was nothing to be done I turned upstream to find a shallower and a safer crossing.

At best it was not pleasant. The water was waist-high and racing in narrow channels between and over boulders and loose slippery stones, and I was glad to get through without a tumble and a swim.

The country was rough on the other side, and the old grass was high and dense, for no one went there in those days, and the grass stood unburnt from season to season.

242

Climbing over rocks and stony ground, crunching dry sticks underfoot, and driving a path through the rank tambookie grass, it seemed wellnigh hopeless to look for a shot. Several times I heard buck start up and dash off only a few metres away, and it began to look as if the wiser course would be to turn back.

At last I got out of the valley into more level and more open ground, and came out upon a ledge or plateau a hundred metres or more wide, with a low ridge of rocks and some thorns on the far side — quite a likely spot. I searched the open ground from my cover, and seeing nothing there crossed over to the rocks, threading my way silently between them and expecting to find another clear space beyond. The snort of a buck brought me to a standstill among the rocks, and as I listened it was followed by another and another from the same quarter, delivered at irregular intervals. Each snort was accompanied by the sound of trampling feet, sometimes like stamps of anger and at other times seemingly a hasty movement.

I had on several occasions interrupted fights between angry rivals. Once two splendid kudu bulls were at it. A second time it was two sables, and the vicious and incredibly swift sweep of the scimitar horns still lives in memory, along with the wonderful nimbleness of the other fellow who dodged it. And another time they were blue wildebeest. But some interruption had occurred each time, and I had no more than a glimpse of what might have been a rare scene to witness.

I was determined not to spoil it this time. No doubt it was a fight, and probably they were fencing and circling for an opening, as there was no bump of heads or clash of horns and no tearing scramble of feet to indicate the real struggle. I crept on through the rocks and found before me a tangle of thorns and dead wood, impossible to pass through in silence. It was better to work back again and try the other side of the rocks.

The way was clearer there, and I crept up to a rock one or two metres high, feeling certain from the sound that the fight would be in full view a few metres beyond. With the rifle ready I raised myself slowly until my eyes were over the top of the rock. Some twenty metres off, in an open flat of downtrodden grass, I saw a sable cow. She was standing with feet firmly and widely planted, looking fiercely in front of her, ducking her head in a threatening manner every few seconds, and giving angry snorts. Behind, and huddled up against her, was her scared bewildered little red-brown calf.

It seemed stupid not to have guessed what it all meant, yet the fact is that for the few remaining seconds I was simply puzzled and fascinated by the behaviour of the two sables. Then in the corner of my eye I saw, away on my right, another red-brown thing come into the open. It was Jock, casting about with nose to ground for my trail which he had overrun at the point where I had turned back near the dead wood on the other side of the rocks.

What happened then was a matter of a second or two. As I turned to look at him he raised his head, bristled up all over, and made one jump forward. Then a long low yellowish thing moved in the unbeaten grass in front of the sable cow, raised its head sharply, and looked full into my eyes. Before I could move a finger it shot away in one streak-like bound.

I took a wild shot at the lioness, as I jumped up full height, and shouted at Jock to come back. There was a scramble of black and brown on my left, and it was all over. I was standing in the open ground, breathless with excitement, and Jock, a few metres off, with hind legs crouched ready for a dash, was looking back at me for leave to go.

The spoor told the tale. There was the outer circle made by the lioness in the grass, broken in places where she had feinted to rush in and stopped before the lowered horns. And inside this there was the smaller circle, a tangle of trampled grass and spoor, where the brave mother had stood between her young and death.

Any attempt to follow the lioness after that would have been waste of time. We struck off in a new direction, and in crossing a stretch of level ground where the thorn trees were well scattered and the grass fairly short, my eye caught a movement in front that brought me to an instant standstill. It was as if the stem of a young thorn tree had suddenly waved itself and settled back again, and it meant that some long-horned buck, perhaps a kudu or a sable bull, was lying

244

down and had swung his head. It meant also that he was comfortably settled, quite unconscious of danger.

I marked and watched the spot, or rather, the line, for the glimpse was too brief to tell more than the direction; but there was no other move. The air was almost still, with just a faint drift from him to us, and I examined every stick and branch, every stump and antheap, every bush and tussock, without stirring a foot. But I could make out nothing. I could trace no outline and see no patch of colour, dark or light, to betray him.

It was an incident very characteristic of bushveld hunting. There I stood minute after minute — not risking a move, which would be certain to reveal me — staring and searching for some big animal lying half-asleep within eighty metres of me on ground that you would not call good cover for a rabbit. We were in the sunlight and he lay somewhere beyond, where a few scattered thorn trees threw dabs of shade, marbling with dappled shade and light the already mottled surface of earth and grass.

I was hopelessly beaten, but Jock could see him well enough. He crouched beside me with ears cocked, and his eyes, all ablaze, were fixed intently on the spot. His hind legs were tucked under him and he was trembling with excitement. Only those will realise it who have been through the tantalising humiliating experience. There was nothing to be done but wait, leaving the buck to make the first move.

245

And at last it came. There was another slight shake of the horns, and the whole figure stood out in bold relief. It was a fine sable bull lying in the shadow of one of the thorn trees with his back towards us, and there was a small antheap close behind him, making a greyish blot against his black back and shoulder, and breaking the expanse of colour which the eye would otherwise easily have picked up.

The antheap made a certain shot impossible, so I lowered myself slowly to the ground to wait until he should begin feeding or change his position for comfort or shade, as they often do. This might mean waiting for half an hour or more, but it was better than risking a shot in the position in which he was lying. I settled down for a long wait with the rifle resting on my knees, confidently expecting that when the time came to move he would get up slowly, stretch himself, and have a good look round. But he did nothing of the kind. A turn or eddy of the faint breeze must have given him my wind. There was one twitch of the horns, as his nose was laid to windward, and without an instant's pause he dashed off. It was the quickest thing imaginable in a big animal. It looked as though he started racing from his lying position. The bush was not close enough to save him, however, in spite of his start, and through the thin veil of smoke I saw him plunge and stumble, and then dash off again. Jock, seeing me give chase, went ahead and in half a minute I was left well behind, but still in sight of the hunt.

I shouted at Jock to come back, just as one murmurs

246

good-day to a passing friend in the din of traffic — from force of habit. Of course, he could hear nothing. It was his first and only go at a sable. He knew nothing of the terrible horns and the deadly scythe-like sweep that makes the wounded sable so dangerous — even the lioness had fought shy of them — and great as was my faith in him, the risk in this case was not one I would have taken. There was nothing to do but follow.

A half a kilometre on I drew closer and found them standing face to face among the thorns. It was the first of three or four stands. The sable, with a watchful eye on me, always moved on as I drew near enough to shoot. The beautiful black and white bull stood facing his little red enemy and the fence and play of feint and thrust, guard and dodge, was wonderful to see. Not once did either touch the other. At Jock's least movement the sable's head would go down with his nose into his chest and the magnificent horns would arch forward poised so as to strike either right or left, and if Jock feinted a rush either way the scythe-sweep came with lightning quickness, covering more than half a circle and carrying the gleaming points with a swing right over the sable's own back. Then he would advance slowly and menacingly, with horns well forward ready to strike and eyes blazing through his eyebrows, driving Jock before him.

It must have been at the fourth or fifth stand that Jock got through the guard at last. The sable was badly wounded in the body and doubtless strength was failing, but there was little evidence of this yet.

This time the sable drove him steadily back towards a big thorn tree, but in the last step, just as the bull made his rush,

247

Jock jumped past the tree and instead of scrambling back out of reach as before, dodged round and was in the rear of the buck before it could turn on him. There were no flying heels to fear then, and without an instant's hesitation he fastened on one of the hind legs above the hock. With a snort of rage and indignation the sable spun round and round, kicking and plunging wildly and making vicious sweeps with his horns. But Jock, although swung about and shaken like a rat, was out of reach, and kept his grip. It was a quick and furious struggle, in which I was altogether forgotten, and as one more desperate plunge brought the bull down in a struggling kicking heap with Jock completely hidden under him, I ran up and ended the fight.

It always took Jock some time to calm down after these tussles. He became so wound up by the excitement of the struggle that time was needed to run down again, so to say. While I was busy on the double precaution of fixing up a scare for the aasvogels and cutting grass and branches to cover the buck, Jock moved restlessly round the sable, ever ready to pounce on him again at the least sign of life. The slithering tongue and wide-open mouth looked like a big red gash splitting his head in two. He was so blown, his breath came and went like the puffing of a diminutive steam-engine at full speed, and his eyes with all the wickedness of fight — but none of the watchfulness — gone out of them, flickered incessantly from the buck to me. One sign from either would have been enough. It was the same old scene, the same old performance, that I had watched scores of times, but it never grew stale or failed to draw a laugh, a word of cheer, and pat of affection. And from him there came always the same response, the friendly wagging of that stumpy tail, a splashy lick, a soft upward look, and a wider split of the mouth that was a laugh as plain as if one heard it.

I was still laughing at him, when he stopped and turning sharply round made a snap at his side. A few seconds later he did it again. Then there was a thin sing of insect wings, and I knew that the tsetse fly were on us.

The only thought then was for Jock, who was still working busily round the sable. For some minutes I sat with him between my legs, wisping away the flies with a small branch and wondering what to do. It soon became clear that there was nothing to be gained by waiting. Instead of passing away the fly became more numerous, and there was not a moment's peace or comfort to be had, for they were tackling me on the neck, arms and legs, where the thorn-ripped pants left me bare to the knees. So, slinging the rifle over my shoulder, I picked Jock up, greatly to his discomfort, and carried him off in my arms at the best pace possible under the circumstances. A kilometre of that was enough, however. A tumble into a grass-hidden hole laid us both out sprawling, and I sat down again to rest and think, swishing the flies off as before.

Then an idea came which, in spite of all the anxiety, made me laugh, and ended in putting poor old Jock in quite the most undignified and ridiculous plight.

I ripped off as much of my shirt as was not needed to protect me against the flies, and making holes in it for his legs and tail fitted him out with a home-made suit in about five minutes. Time was everything. It was impossible to run with him in my arms, but we could run together until we got out of the fly belt, and there was not much risk of being bitten as long as we kept up the running in the long grass. It was a long spell, and what with the rough country and the uncontrollable laughter at the sight of Jock, I was pretty well done by the time we were safely out of the fly. We pulled up when the country began to fall away sharply towards the river, and there, to Jock's evident satisfaction, I took off his suit — by that time very much tattered and awry.

It was there, lying between two rocks in the shade of a marula tree, that I got one of those chances to see game at close quarters of which most men only hear or dream. There were no snapshot cameras then.

We had been lying there it may be for half an hour or

249

more, Jock asleep and I spread out on my back, when a slight but distinct click, as of a hoof against a stone, made me turn quietly over on my side and listen. The rock beside me was about one metre high, and on the other side of it a buck of some kind, and a big one too, was walking with easy stride towards the river.

The footsteps came abreast of us and then stopped. The sudden halt seemed to mean that some warning instinct had arrested him, or some least taint upon the pure air softly eddying between the rocks had reached him. I could hear his sniffs, and pictured him looking about, silent but alarmed, before deciding which way to make his rush.

I raised myself bit by bit, close to the rock, until I could see over it. A magnificent waterbuck bull, full-grown and in perfect coat and condition, was standing less than five metres away and a little to the right, having already passed me when he came to a stop. He was so close that I could see the waves and partings in his heavy coat, the rise and fall in his flanks as he breathed, the ruff on his shaggy bearded throat, and the nostrils, mobile and sensitive, searching for the least hint of danger. The eye, large and full and soft, was luminous with watchful intelligence, and yet mild and calm — so free was it from all trace of a disturbing thought. I was so close, it seemed almost possible to reach out and touch him. There was no thought of shooting. It was a moment of supreme enjoyment. Just to watch him was enough.

In a little while he seemed satisfied that all was well, and with head thrown slightly forward and the sure clean tread of his kind, he took his line unhesitatingly down the hill. As he neared the thicker bush twenty metres away a sudden impulse made me give a shout. In a single bound he was lost among the trees, and the clattering of loose stones and the crackle of sticks in his path had ceased before the cold shiver down the back, which my spell-breaking shout provoked, had passed away. When I turned round Jock was still asleep. Little incidents like that brought his deafness home.

It was our last day's hunting together, and I went back to the dreary round of hard, hopeless, useless struggle and daily loss.

250

There were only twenty oxen left when we reached the drift below Fig Tree. The water was nearly breast-high and we carried three-fourths of the loads through on our heads, case by case, to make the pull as easy as possible for the oxen.

We got one wagon through with some difficulty, but at nightfall the second was still in the river. We had carried out everything removable, even to the buck-sails, but the weakened bullocks could not move the empty wagon.

The thunder-clouds were piling up ahead, and distant lightning gave warning of a storm away up river; so we wound the trek-chain round a big tree on the bank, to anchor the wagon in case of flood. Reeling from work and weariness, too tired to think of food, I flung myself down in my blankets under the other wagon which was outspanned where we had stopped it in the double-rutted veld road, and settling comfortably into the sandy furrow cut by many wheels, was 'dead to the world' in a few minutes. Near midnight the storm awoke me and a curious coldness about the neck and shoulders made me turn over to pull the blankets up. The road had served as a storm-water drain, converting the two wheel furrows into running streams, and I, rolled in my blankets, had dammed up one of them. The prompt flow of the released water as soon as I turned over, told plainly what had happened. I looked out at the driving rain and the glistening earth, as shown up by constant flashes of lightning. It was a world of rain and spray and running water. It seemed that there was neither hope nor mercy anywhere. I was too tired to care, and dropping back into the trough, slept the night out in water.

In the morning we found the wagon still in the drift, al-though partly hidden by the flood, but the force of the stream had half-floated and half-forced it round on to higher ground; and only the anchoring chain had saved it. We had to wait some hours for the river to run down, and then to my relief the rested but staggering oxen pulled it out at the first attempt.

Rooiland, the light red ox with blazing yellow eyes and topped horns, fierce and untameable to the end, was in the lead then. I saw him as he took the strain in that last pull,

and it was pitiful to see the restless eager spirit fighting against the failing strength. He looked desperate. The thought seems fanciful and perhaps it is, but what happened just afterwards makes it still vivid and it fitted in very curiously with the superstitious notions of the drivers.

We outspanned in order to repack the loads, and Rooiland, who as front ox was the last to be released, stood for a few moments alone while the rest of the cattle moved away. Then turning his back on them he gave a couple of low moaning bellows and walked down the road back to the drift again. The wagon drivers stopped their work and watched him curiously, and some remarks passed which were inaudible to me. As the ox disappeared down the slope into the drift, Jim called to his leader to bring him back, and then turning to me, added with his usual positiveness, 'Rooiland is mad. Umtagati! Bewitched! He is looking for the dead ones. He is going to die today!'

The leader came back presently alone. When he reached the drift, Rooiland was standing breast-high in the river, and then in a moment, whether by step or slip, he was into the flood and swept away. The leader's account was received by the others in absolute silence. A little tightening of the jaws and a little brightening of the eyes were all I could detect. They accepted the position without a word. I suggested to Jim that it was nothing but a return of Rooiland's old straying habit, and probed him with questions, but could get nothing out of him. Finally he walked off with an expensive shake of the head and the repetition of his former remark,

252

without a shade of triumph, surprise, or excitement in his voice: 'He is looking for the dead ones.'

We were out of the fly then, and the next day we reached Fig Tree.

That was the end of the last trek. Only three oxen reached Barberton, and they died within the week. The ruin was complete.

Our Various Ways

When the trip was squared off and the drivers paid, there was nothing left. Jim went home with some wagons returning to Spitzkop. Once more, but for the last time, he was grievously hurt in dignity because his money was handed to my friend, the owner of the wagons, to be paid out to him when he reached his kraal. But his gloomy resentment melted as I handed over to him the things for which I had no further need.

The wagons moved off, and Jim with them, but twice he broke back again to dance and shout his gratitude. It was wealth to him to have the reims and voorslag, the odd yokes and strops and wagon tools, the baking pot and pan and billies. Jim, with all his faults, had earned some title to remembrance for his loyalty. My way had been his way, and the hardest day had never been too hard for him. He had seen it all through to the finish, without a grumble and without a shirk.

His last shout, like the bellow of a bull, was an uproarious goodbye to Jock. And Jock seemed to know it was something of an occasion, for, as he stood before me looking down the road at the receding wagons and the dancing figure of Jim, his ears were cocked, his head was tilted a little sideways, and his tail stirred gently. It was at least a friendly nod in return.

So the new life began and the old was put away. But the new life, for all its brighter and wider outlook and work of another class, for all the charm that makes Barberton now a cherished memory to all who knew the early days, was not all happy. The new life had its hours of darkness too. Hours of almost unbearable 'trek fever', of restless, sleepless longing for the old life, of 'homesickness' for the veld, the freedom, the roaming, the nights by the fire, and the days in the bush.

All that was left of the old life was Jock, and soon there was no place for him. He could not always be with me, and when left behind he was miserable, leading a life that was utterly strange to him. While I was in Barberton he accompanied me everywhere, but — absurd as it seems — there was a constant danger for him there, greater though less glorious than those he faced so lightly in the veld.

His deafness, which passed almost unnoticed and did not seem to handicap him at all in the veld, became a serious danger in camp. For a long time he had been unable to hear a sound, but he could feel sounds; that is to say, he was quick to notice anything that caused a vibration. In the early days of his deafness I had been worried by the thought that he would be run over while lying asleep near or under the wagons, and the drivers were always on the look-out to stir him up; but we soon found that this was not necessary. At the first movement he would feel the vibration and jump up. He seemed to know the difference between the sounds he could ignore, such as chopping wood, and those that he ought to notice.

In camp — Barberton in those days was reckoned a mining camp, and was always referred to as 'camp' — the danger was due to the number of sounds. He would stand behind me as I stopped in the street, and sometimes lie down and snooze if the wait was a long one. At first he was very watchful, and every rumbling wheel or horse's footfall drew his alert little eyes round to the danger point. But the traffic and noise

255

were almost continuous — one sound ran into another — and he became careless or puzzled and on several occasions narrowly escaped being run over or trodden on.

Once, in desperation after a bad scare, I tried chaining him up, and although his injured reproachful look hurt, it did not weaken me. I had hardened my heart to do it, and it was for his own sake. At lunch-time he was still squatting at the full length of the chain, off the mat and straw, and straw, and with his head hanging in the most hopeless dejected attitude one could imagine. It was too much for me — the dog really felt it. When I released him there was no rejoicing in his freedom. He turned from me without a sign or sound of any sort, and walking off slowly, lay down some ten metres away with his head resting on his paws. He went to think — not to sleep.

I felt abominably guilty, and was conscious of wanting to make up for it all the afternoon.

Once I took him out to Fig Tree Creek twenty five kílometres away, and left him with a prospector friend at whose camp in the hills it seemed he would be much better off and much happier. When I got back to Barberton that night he was waiting for me, with a tag of chewed rope hanging round his neck, not the least ashamed of himself, but openly rejoicing in the meeting and evidently never doubting that I was equally pleased. And he was quite right there.

But it could not go on. One day as he lay asleep behind me, a loaded wagon coming sharply round a corner nearly passed over him. The wheel was centimetres from his back as he lay asleep in the sand. There was no chance to grab — it was a rush and a kick that saved him, and he rolled under the wagon and found his own way out between the wheels.

A few days after this Ted passed through Barberton, and I handed Jock over to him, to keep and to care for until I had a better and safer home for him.

One day some two years later there turned up at my quarters an old friend of the transport days — Harry Williams — he had been away on a long trek 'up north' to look for some supposed mine of fabulous richness of which there had been vague and secret reports. He stayed with me for some days and one evening after a bout of fever and ague had passed off and rest and good feeding had begun to pull him round, he told us the story of their search. It was a trip of much adventure, but it was the end of his story that interested me most, and that is all that need be told here.

They had failed to find the mine. The man who was supposed to know all about it had deserted, with all he could carry off. They were short of food and money. Out of medicines, they were 300 kilometres from any White men. There was no road but their own erratic track through the bush. The rains had begun and the fever season set in. The cattle were worn out; the fever had gripped them, and of the six White men, three were dead, one was dying and two were only able to crawl. The driver — delirious with fever — completed the party.

The long journey was almost over. They were only a few treks from the store and camp for which they were making, but they were so stricken and helpless it seemed as though that little was too much and they must die within reach of help.

The driver, a big Zulu, was then raving mad. He had twice run off into the bush and been lost for hours. Precious time and waning strength were spent in the search, and with infinite effort and much good luck they had found him and induced him to return. On the second occasion they had enticed him on to the wagon, and as he lay half-unconscious between bursts of delirium, had tied him down flat on his back, with wrists and ankles fastened to the buck-rails. From time to time, they climbed up and put water in his mouth. It was all they could do to save him.

It was midday then, and their dying comrade was so far gone that they decided to abandon one trek and wait for evening, to allow him to die in peace. It was then that the man opened his eyes and faintly shook his head; so they inspanned as best they could and made another trek.

It was then at most two more treks to their destination, but they were too weak to work or walk, and the cattle were left to crawl along undriven. After half an hour's trekking they reached a bad drift where the wagon stuck. The cattle would not face the pull. The two tottering, trembling White men did their best, but neither had the strength to use the whip.

The water had given out, and the despairing helpless men saw death from thirst awaiting them within a few hours' trek of help. To add to the horror of it all the Zulu driver, with thirst aggravating his delirium, was a raving lunatic — struggling and wrenching at his bonds until the wagon rattled.

Hours had gone by in hopeless effort, but the oxen stood out at all angles, and no two would pull together in answer to the feeble efforts of the fainting men. Then there came a lull in the shouts from the wagon and in answer to the little voorloper's warning shout, 'Pas op, Baas!' (Look out, Master!) the White men looked round and saw the Zulu driver up on his knees freeing himself from the reims. In another moment he was standing up full height — a magnificent but most unwelcome sight.

There was a thin line of froth along the half-opened mouth and the deep-set eyes glared as for a few seconds he leaned forward like a lion about to spring. As they watched him in breathless silence, he sprang lightly off the wagon, picked up a small dry stick as he landed, and ran up along the span.

He spoke to the after-ox by name as he passed it. Called to another, and touched it into place. He thrust his way between the next one and the dazed White man standing near it, tossing him aside with a brush of his arm. Then they saw how the man's madness had taken him. His work and his span had called to him in his delirium; and he had answered. With low mutterings, short words hissed out, and all the sounds and terms the cattle knew shot at them — low pitched and with intense repression — he ran along the span, crouching low all the time.

Reaching the front oxen, he grasped the leading reim and pulled them round until they stood level for the straight pull out. Down the other side of the span he ran with cat-like tread and activity, talking to each and straightening them up as he had done with the others. When he reached the wagon again, he turned sharply and overlooked the span. One ox had swung round and stood out of line. There was a pause of seconds, and then the big Zulu called to the ox by name — not loudly but in a deep low tone, husky with intensity — and the animal swung back into line again.

Then out of the silence that followed came an electrifying yell to the span. Every bullock leaned to its yoke, and the wagon went out with a rush.

And he drove them at a half-trot all the way to the store. Without water; without help; without consciousness; the little dry twig still in his hand, and only his masterful intensity and knowledge of his work and span to see him through.

'A mad troublesome savage', said Harry Williams, 'but one of the very best. Anyhow, we thought so. He saved us!'

There was something very familiar in this, and it was with a queer feeling of pride and excitement that I asked, 'Did he ever say to you, "My catchum lion 'live"?'

'By gum! You know him? Jim. Jim Makokel'!'

'Indeed I do. Good old Jim.'

259

His Duty

And Jock?

But I never saw my dog again. For a year or so he lived something of the old veld life, trekking and hunting. From time to time I heard of him from Ted and others. Stories seemed to gather easily about him as they do about certain people, and many knew Jock and were glad to bring news of him. The things they thought wonderful and admirable made pleasant news for them to tell and welcome news to me, and they were heard with contented pride, but without surprise.

One day I received word from Ted that he was off to Scotland for a few months and had left Jock with another old friend, Tom Barnett. For a few months it would not matter, but I had no idea of letting Jock end his days as a watch-dog at a trader's store.

When Jock saw or scented the thieves and the mongrel dogs that used to sneak into Tom's store and his house stealing everything they could get he fought to kill, and not as town dogs fight. He had learnt his work in a hard school, and he never stopped or slackened until the work was done. So his fame soon spread and it brought Tom more peace than he had enjoyed for many a day.

However, things did not always work out so simply at night. The dogs from the surrounding kraals prowled about scavenging and thieving and, what angered Tom most of all, killing his fowls. The yard at the back of the store was enclosed by a fence of reeds, and in the middle of the yard stood the fowl house with a clear space of bare ground all round it. On many occasions dogs had found their way through the reed fence and killed fowls perching about the yard, and several times they had burgled the fowl house itself. In spite of Jock's presence and reputation, this night robbing still continued, for while he slept peacefully in front of the store, the robbers would do their work at the back. Poor old fellow. They were many and he was one. They prowled night and day and he had to sleep sometimes. They were watchful and he was deaf. So, he had no chance at all unless he saw or scented them.

There were two small windows looking out on to the yard, but no door in the back of the building. Thus, in order to get into the yard, it was necessary to go out of the front door and round the side of the house. On many occasions Tom, roused by the screaming of the fowls, had seized his gun and run round to get a shot at the thieves; but the time so lost was enough for the dog, and the noise made in opening the reed gate gave ample warning of his coming.

The result was that Tom generally had all his trouble for nothing. But it was not always so. Several times he roused Jock as he ran out, and invariably got some satisfaction out of what followed. Once Jock caught one of the thieves struggling to force a way through the fence and held on to the hind leg until Tom came up with the gun. On other occasions he had caught them in the yard, or had run them down in the bush and finished it off there without help or hindrance.

That was the kind of life to which Jock seemed to have settled down.

He was then in the very prime of life, and I still hoped to get him back to me some day to a home where he would end his days in peace. Yet it seemed impossible to picture him in a life of ease and idleness — a watch-dog living in a house, sleeping away his life on a mat; his only excitement keeping

off strange men and stray dogs, or burrowing for rats and moles in a garden; with old age, deafness, and infirmities growing year by year to make his end miserable. I had often thought that it might have been better had he died fighting.

Well, Jock is dead. Jock, the innocent cause of Seedling's downfall and death, lies buried under the same big fig tree. The graves stand side by side. He died, as he lived — true to his trust. This is how it happened, as it was faithfully told to me:

It was a bright moonlight night — think of the scores we had spent together, the mild glorious nights of the bush-veld — and once more Tom was roused by a clatter of falling boxes and the wild screams of fowls in the yard. Only the night before the thieves had beaten him again, but this time he was determined to get even with them. Jumping out of bed he opened the little window looking out on to the fowl house, and, with his gun resting on the sill, waited for the thief. He waited long and patiently. By and by the screaming of the fowls subsided enough for him to hear the gurgling and scratching about in the fowl house, and he settled down to a still longer watch. Evidently the dog was enjoying his stolen meal in there.

'Go on! Finish it!' Tom muttered grimly; 'I'll have you this time if I wait till morning!'

So he stood at the window waiting and watching, until every sound had died away outside. He listened intently. There was not a stir. There was nothing to be seen in the moonlit yard, nothing to be heard, not even a breath of air to rustle the leaves in the big fig tree.

Then, in the same dead stillness the dim form of a dog appeared in the doorway, stepped softly out of the fowl house, and stood in the deep shadow of the little porch.

Tom lifted the gun slowly and took careful aim. When the smoke cleared away, the figure of the dog lay still, stretched out on the ground where it had stood. Tom went back to bed, satisfied.

The morning sun slanting across the yard shone in Tom's eyes as he pushed the reed gate open and made his way towards the fowl house. Under the porch where the sunlight touched it, something shone like burnished gold.

He was stretched on his side — it might have been in sleep. But on the snow-white chest there was one red spot. And inside the fowl house lay the thieving dog — dead.

Jock had done his duty.

A Glossary of Bushveld Terms

(Current spellings in parantheses)

Aasvogel (Aasvoël). A vulture.

Antheap. Mound made by termites or 'white ants'. Usually about 0,6—1,2 metres in base diameter and height, but sometimes up to 5,4 metres in diameter in certain localities. Hollowed out by early pioneers to use as bake ovens.

Assegai. An African's spear, used in hunting and war.

Baas. Master. Mode of address used by non-Whites to employer.

Billy. A small tin utensil with lid and handle, used for boiling water.

Biltong. Meat cut in strips, slightly salted, and dried in the open air.

Bucksail. Tarpaulin used for covering transport wagons, which are known as buckwagons.

Bushbuck. A medium-sized but very courageous antelope.

Bushveld. Bush country, often thorny, scrubby; also called lowveld and low country.

Cetywayo, Ketshwayo (Cetshwayo). Fourth and last of the great Zulu kings.

Chaka (Shaka). The first of the great Zulu kings and founder of the Zulu military power.

Dassie. Rock rabbit.

Dingaan (Dingane). The second of the great Zulu kings; brother, murderer, and successor of Shaka.

Disselboom. The pole of an ox wagon.

Donga. A gully or dry watercourse with steep banks.

Double span. To double the number of oxen pulling a wagon.

Doughboys. Scones; frequently unleavened dough baked in coals; also, askoeks, roosterkoekies, stick-in-the-gizzards, veld-bricks.

Drift. A ford.

Duiker. A small antelope found throughout Africa.

Go'way bird. The grey plantain eater.

Hartebeeste (Hartebeest). A large antelope.

Highveld. High country; the plateau, about 1 500 to 2 000 metres above sea-level.

Honey bird. The honey-guide.

Honey sucker. Sun-bird.

Horse sickness. A lung infection prevalent during summer in low-lying parts; generally fatal. Caused by microbes introduced in the blood by some insect.

Hottentot god (Hottentotsgot). A praying mantis.

Impala. A large and common antelope; habitat, bushveld.

Impi. An army or body of armed African men gathered for or engaged in war.

Induna. A headman, captain, or chief, great or petty.

Inkos (Inkosi). Chief; used as a term of respect in address or salutation.

Inspan. To yoke up, harness up, or hitch up animals at the beginning of a journey.

Isandhlwana (Isandlwana) (pro. saan-shle-waá-na). Meaning 'the little hand'; the hill which gave the name to the battle in which the 24th Regiment was annihilated in the Zulu War, 1879.

Kahle (pro. kaa-shle). Exclamation of caution. Gently, carefully, pleasantly, well. 'Hamba kahle', farewell, go in peace. 'Hlala (pro. shlala) kahle', farewell, stay in peace.

Kehla (pro. keh-shlaa). An African man of certain age and position entitled to wear the headring.

Kerrie (kierie). Sticks used for fighting and frequently knobbed; hence, knob-kerrie.

Klipspringer. A small mountain antelope.

Kloof. A gorge between mountains. A deep, often wooded, ravine.

Kopje (koppie). A hill, flat-topped or pointed.

Kraal (pro. crawl). An enclosure for cattle, sheep; a corral; also a collection of huts, the home of a family, the village of a chief.

Krans. A precipitous face or coronet of rock on a hill or mountain, often overlooking a river.

Kudu. Large antelope with great curling horns. Habitat, rugged bush country.

Lagavaan (Leguaan) (Likkewaan). A huge water lizard, the monitor. Maximum length up to 2,4 metres.

Looper. Round shot for fowling piece, about four times the size of buckshot.

Marula, in Zulu *Umgano.* A tree which furnishes soft white wood, which is carved into bowls, spoons; fruit eaten or fermented for drink.

Meerkat. A small animal of the mongoose kind.

Middleveld. The mixed country lying between the highveld and the bushveld.

Nek-strop. The neck strap, or reim, which, attached to the yokeskeys, keeps the yoke in place.

Oribi. A small antelope.

Outspan. To unyoke or unharness; also the camp where one has outspanned, and places where it is customary or by law permitted to outspan.

Panda (Mpande). The third of the great Zulu kings.

Partridge, Pheasant. Names applied somewhat loosely to various species of francolin.

Pauw (Pou). The great South African bustard.

Poort. A gap or gorge in a range of hills.

Reim (Riem). A stout strip of rawhide.

Rietbuck (Rietbok) (Reedbuck). A small South African antelope.

Sakubona. Zulu equivalent of 'Good Day'.

Salted Horse. One which has had horse sickness, and is thus considered immune; hence 'salted' is freely used colloquially as meaning acclimatised, tough, hardened.

Schans (pro. skaans). A stone or earth breastwork for defence, very common in old wars.

Schelm (Skelm). A rascal, villain.

Scherm (Skerm) (pro. skarem). A protection of bush or trees, usually against wild animals.

Sjambok (pro. shambok). Tapering rawhide whip made from rhinoceros, hippopotamus, or giraffe skin.

Sloot (pro. slooh-rt). A man-made ditch for water supply.

Span. A team of oxen or other draught animals.

Spoor. Footprints; also a trail of man, animal, or vehicle.

Springbuck (Springbok). A small, swift antelope.

Spruit (pro. sprait). A stream.

Stembuck (Steenbok) (pro. stearn-bok). Small antelope of the genus *Nanotragus (tragulus),* literally 'stone buck'.

Stoep. A raised promenade or paved veranda in front or at the sides of a house.

Tambuki Grass, also *Tambookie (Tamboekie).* A very rank grass, in places reaches 4,5 metres high.

Tick, or *Rhinoceros, Bird.* The ox-pecker.

Tock-Tockie (Toktokkie). A blackish, slow-moving beetle, incapable of flight. Gets its name from its means of signalling by rapping the abdomen on the ground.

Trek. To move off or go on a journey. A journey, an expedition; also, and commonly, the time, distance, or journey from one outspan to another.

Tsessebe. An antelope, one of the hartebeest family.

Tsetse Fly. A grey fly, little larger than the common housefly, whose bite transmits sleeping sickness to man and is almost always fatal to domesticated animals.

Twiggle. Little people's word for the excited movement of a small dog's tail, believed to be a combination of wriggle and twiddle.

Umfaan. Zulu: young, African boy.

Umganaam. Zulu: my friend.

Umlungu. The Black man's word to describe a White man. (Now often ironic).

Veld. The open or unoccupied country; uncultivated or grazing land.-

Vlei (pro. flay). A small, shallow lake, a swamp, a depression intermittently damp, a water meadow.

Voorlooper (Voorloper). The leader, the young boy who leads the front oxen.

Voorslag (pro. foor-slaach). The strip of buck hide which forms the fine end of a whip-lash.

Wildebeeste (Wildebees) (pro. vill-de-beast). The brindled gnu, blue wildebeest.

Wild Dog. The 'Cape hunting dog'. Predatory; hunts in packs; destroys both flocks and game.

Wooden Orange. Fruit of the klapper; monkey orange.

Wolf. The usual name for the hyena.

Yokeskey (Jukskei). The wooden slat which, coupled by nek-strops, holds the yoke in place.